D0829813

THE PITCHER'S MOM

Heather Choate Davis

STEWART PRESS

THE PITCHER'S MOM

All rights reserved.

Copyright © 2012 by Heather Choate Davis and Stewart Press. No part of this book may be used or reproduced in any manner whatsoever without written permission except in the case of brief quotations embodied in articles and reviews.

ISBN: 978-0-9853504-8-2

For all the moms who give their hearts
to the big dream of baseball.

"I don't know why he'd say
something like that."

Two by two the parents arrived to perch on the tiny seats upon which their children had, for the past three years, eaten their apple slices and laid the foundations for their stunning and singular futures. Jill put her jacket on the empty chair beside her and studied the wall where the children's art was displayed. There were rainbows and balloons. There were smiley faces with loop-de-loop hair. Some of the girls were already drawing real cats and signing their work in near cursive. Not Gus. Gus's magnum opus was his name writ large in tempera blue and underlined with a slapdash brush stroke that ran clear off the page and right out the door to play. A minimalist Jill sighed as the preschool director clapped her hands and a tinny, boom-boxed "Pomp and Circumstance" summoned the graduates to process.

Kailey S. was the line leader. As if to her own coronation she approached, her pigtailed head held like a cameo pin as her classmates wriggled and teemed like road blocked ants behind her. On a wave of rebellious murmurs, Gus made his move, storming the passing lane with restless, confident strides. Kailey S. scowled and held out her arm to block him.

"Well, hurry up wouldja," Gus whispered loudly.

All the parents laughed. All but Kailey's mother who, with an uncannily similar whip of the head, turned back towards Jill and scowled in kind. What did Mrs. S. expect? Didn't she know that boys don't like to stand around? That boys don't like to take contrived baby steps when one giant leap would get them there faster, better.

At the far end of the room, napping mats were stacked like risers upon which the young graduates aligned themselves. Mortarboards slipping off their lice-free heads, they stepped forward to declare their plans for the future. "My name is Annalisa La Pietro and I want to be a veterinarian."

All eyes turned toward Annalisa's proud father and mother who said demurely, to the parents on either side, "She always has had a way with animals."

Max wanted to be a business manager like his dad. Logan, a tax attorney like her mother. A tiny boy in suspenders with a holstered sword fancied himself a dragon slayer— a quest that seemed perfectly enchanting to his aging, beatnik moms. Jill hoped Gus would say poet. Poet or playwright or, despite all evidence to the contrary, painter.

There was one more boy in front of Gus. Jill found herself lurching for a scrap of paper and a pen. Just a last minute suggestion. Something short. Something easy to read. A nice, familiar three letter word he could say without stumbling if she held it up over her head; my name is Gus Oberdorf and I want to be a C-A-T when I grow up.

"My name is Caleb Zeus Holstein-Deerborne," the next boy lisped. He traced the floor with anemic, low-slung eyes as the microphone spat out his esses. "And I want to be a particle physicist."

Jill unclicked her pen. A person's calling was a private—some would even say sacred—matter. It whispered in young ears, guiding willing souls like a pillar of cloud, until time and circumstance at last forged a union of glimmer and flesh. It was not a subject for public spectacle.

All eyes were now on Gus. Physically speaking he was medium in almost every way. Medium height, medium build, his hair and eyes medium brown. The most spectacular thing about his physical presence was the ease he seemed to feel in his own skin. Gus slid his hands nonchalantly into his pockets and a collective slackening could be felt across the knotted shoulders of the overachieving crowd. Even Jill loosened her grip on the camera. He was, after all, only five. So what if he said ninja fighter. Or race car driver. Or singer in a rock n' roll band. Whatever it was, it was hardly binding.

With an unnerving lack of hesitation, he spoke. "My name is Gus Oberdorf. And I'm going to be a professional baseball player."

At the sound of his words the very fabric of time was ripped open and laid bare. Blood pelted Jill's eardrums, her temples, her cheeks. Air, sound, breath, light, all were frozen instantly, as the question of where on earth her son would get an idea like that resounded in the cosmic pause.

A man leaned over the empty seat beside her and said, "Tell Gus we'll be on the look out for him at Dodger Stadium."

Jill flinched and, in a tone usually reserved for the denial of firearms, replied, "I don't know why he'd say something like that. We don't even own a baseball."

Now we do.

Gus's birthday was three weeks later. Jill was hard-pressed to come up with a reason not to give him what he wanted. It wasn't a party or a puppy or a trip to the moon. It wasn't even expensive. After a traditional Oberdorf birthday breakfast of strudel and kielbasa and chocolate milk, Jill sat him down in the big red chair in the living room. On special occasions it doubled as a throne. Handing him his first present, Jill bowed. "Your six-year-oldness..."

Gus felt his way around the book-shaped gift and reluctantly peeled back the wrapping. "They're French warrior sonnets," Jill said, as if that fact would make all the difference. "They're just loaded with sword fights and cannonballs and all sorts of great boy adventures." Gus looked at the cover— at the man in the tights and the pointed, feathered cap— then back at his mother, who sputtered, "The guy at the campus bookstore said it was a really good translation." How hopeful she had been in that moment, when her latest plan to slay her son's resistance to all manner of text had first been hatched. "I just thought maybe we could start a special summer routine. Read a few verses each day."

"Ya mean today?!"

"No. Of course not." Wistfully setting the book aside, Jill said, "On second thought, maybe we'll just save them till

9

you're a little bit older."

The smile she'd foolishly hoped to receive for the anthology came instead with the decision to shelve it. Reaching for the second box, Gus gave it an optimistic shake—

"Stop! It's fragile."

Even unwrapped, Gus was unsure of what it was. "It's a microscope," Jill explained. "It's for looking close up at bugs and leaves and things." In truth, he'd shown about as much interest in bugs and leaves as he had in books. Resorting to name dropping, Jill said, "It's the same kind they use at NASA. Only, you know, not quite as powerful."

"Gee, thanks." Gus set the microscope on the French warrior in tights and said, "You remember I gave you a list, right?"

"Did you?"

"Mo-om."

"Hm. I think you're right. I think there is one more thing. Now, where did I put it?" From the broom closet in the hallway, Jill unearthed the long, tubular, ribbon-topped package. Gus leapt to his feet as his mother approached, each of them beaming, he at the shape of the gift, she at the delight in his man-child eyes. It was not until she placed the wrapped bat down in his hands—in the exact instant when the package left her grip and rested wholly in his—that a nearly imperceptible shadow passed over his brow.

"Gussy, what's wrong?"

Too quickly he said, "Nothing."

The plastic bat and wiffle ball set were revealed with a single-tear of the wrapping, a special-edition paper with the pennants of all the Major League Baseball teams: Jill had gone to three stores just to find it. "Are you sure?"

Gus stroked the thin, raised seams of the molded bat. "It's great, mom. It's just want I wanted. Really." With feigned heft he lifted it up over his right shoulder and, waggling it plausibly said, again and again throughout the day until Jill had no choice but to believe him, "Really."

Not exactly a sports girl.

In the fall of her 9th-grade year at North Canton High School, Jill and sports had reached an impasse. The game was soccer, but it could just as well have been cricket or softball or capture the flag. Surrounded by a crowd of sweaty, madly-shouting peers, their eyes abulge with predatorial glee, Jill instinctively retreated to a quieter place. A place where she was free to daydream about the characters she'd left on her night stand; about the long, meandering walk home, the burnt color of the autumn leaves, the tangy sweetness of the Orange Crush that she planned to buy at the corner –

THUMP! A ball kicked cross field hit her temple with a watermelon thud. Jill lay sprawled in the soft, moist grass. The dewy, sun-kissed grass. The fresh, green-smelling—no, the green, fresh-smelling—

"Oberdorf, get up!"

Jill's father and mother both worked at the high school, he as a math teacher, she as the Assistant Principal's secretary. Jill was never entirely sure where the idea had come from, but after that day it was somehow decided that her high school phys-ed requirements could be met in the school library with the daily lifting of heavy books, an arrangement Jill likened to serving hard time in Heaven. There in the sublime and ruckusless chamber, she moved through the stacks: From

Aesycles to Dante, Eco to Faulkner, Hugo to Naruda to Plato to Yeats. She liked tragedy more than comedy and stories of star-crossed lovers best of all. She developed, as a junior, a particular obsession with the lives of literary women named Jane: Austen and Hamilton and Smiley, who came to speak at the local library. All the best writers were named Jane, she decided dreamily. Jane or Anne, but if she changed her name to Jane, she could keep her monogram. In the spring of her senior year, with scholarship offers to Weslyan and Yale and, closer to home, Ohio State, she happened upon a dusty copy of *The Arabian Nights*. Convinced that the desert was calling her, the only child of Bert and Marjorie Oberdorf turned her enchanted sights to Tucson, and all the moonlit camel-rides the University of Arizona had to offer.

Two weeks before Jill's first trip home for the winter break, an art class from her high school alma mater took a field trip to the Cleveland Museum. The flu season had struck early that year and chaperons were hard to come by. When the yellow school bus hit a patch of black ice and went nose first into the slushy frost of Portage Lake, Jill's mom and dad were, inexplicably, in the very first seat. "There must be some mistake," Jill said when the pastor of her parents' church called with the news. "My parents don't even like art."

She had been reading *King Lear* at the time, a happenstance she struggled in vain to see as symbolic. She had no siblings. No one to fight with over the modest estate. No one to help her with the arrangements, or shore her up when the weight of independence became unbearable. No one, even now, to call and ask what kind of baseball bat a six-year-old boy might have been expecting.

Batter up!

On a neglected diamond in the neighborhood park where Jill and Gus had once attended Mommy-and-Me Tai Chi, they took their positions. "All right, Mom, just throw it right over the plate."

Jill cupped the ball between her two hands. She pulled her right arm back and, scooping down and out, released the wiffle like a bowling ball. The featherweight, hole-studded orb fluttered and soughed and dropped like a wadded-up burger wrapper before ever reaching the plate. "Sorry, let me move up a little," Jill said. Again she cupped the ball in her hand, withdrew her arm and, with something like uumph, let it fly.

Gus ran up to fetch it, suggested gently, "Maybe you should move up a little more."

"I think that's a good idea." After three tries, Jill arrived at a working distance of eight feet. "All right, this is going to be a good one. Get ready."

"I'm ready."

"Here it comes." With one perfect upward-arcing toss, Jill placed the ball smack dab over the plate. Like cannon fire the wiffle returned. Jill's arms sprung up like snakes in a can as she dropped to the ground, cowering.

"Way to get dirty, mom."

The ball was all the way in the outfield. Jill walked,

then jogged, to retrieve it. Again she threw. And again Gus hit, so hard and fast she began to wonder if maybe foam might have been a better choice. She threw it low, she threw it high, she threw it inside, she threw it out (she had only been trying to throw it straight ahead). Fifty balls, and only once did her son whiff the air. "Did you ever do this at school?"

Gus shook his head and said, "Again."

Jill rubbed her arm. "Just a few more." Toss, duck, whack, fetch; toss, duck, whack, fetch. "I'm getting quite a workout here, buddy. Okay. Last one!" Gus dug his heels into the dusty, summer dirt and stared his mother down. Jill sneered. Gus scowled. Jill rubbed the ball in her hand and spit. "Gross, mom," he said, never taking his eye off the ball, as he directed every ounce of his 65-pound body toward the fences. The sound was not a thud exactly, more of a dull crack, followed by the sight of the wiffle dribbling out like a failed bunt. As if the full cruelty of life had never before this day been apparent to him, Gus gazed at the wounded bat, stroked the gaping, split plastic seam. Jill moved in slowly, wrapping her arm around his knobby shoulders. "I'm sorry, buddy." She considered, briefly, buying a new one, but visions of daily trips to the bat store—of bats on demand like cereal and milk—deterred her. She opted instead to use the faulty equipment as a teaching moment. "Have you ever heard of designed obsolescence?" she asked and, veering off into a litany of examples, gently steered Gus away from the field.

The Tortoises.

An unsuccessful push for tenure kept Jill's mind off baseball through most of Gus's kindergarten year and into the fall of first grade, where circumstances grew so dire there was no possible consideration of extracurricular activities. Despite logic and biology and even justice the boy, who was made up in no small part of her bookish genes, was placed in the reading group known, cruelly, as *The Tortoises*.

A streak of sleepless nights ensued. Alone, over cocoa and the rattle of Santa Ana winds slapping cans across the alley below, Jill pored over Gus's baby journals for answers. She had read to him three times daily, never less than twenty minutes a session. She had taken him to toddler-appropriate enrichment activities (LACMA, MOCA, the Aboriginal Dance Theatre). She had labeled, religiously, every object and concept his young eyes and ears encountered (*wainscotting, chrysanthemum, irony*). Charts, logs, ticket stubs, photos, all the evidence was there: Jill had done everything a good mother is supposed to do to ensure that her son would not only love art, music, culture and the written word, but (oh, let's face it!) would have a leg up on his classmates, as well.

Despite her best efforts, still, they found themselves here, shipwrecked on this inhospitable island. This cold, lonely, fatherless land. During those dark hours, the well-worn cassettes of *Shakespeare for the Very Young* provided Jill's only solace, the lush verses like harp strings to her fretful ears.

It's just a game.

In fits and starts Jill slept, finally bolting upright in the early morning hours empowered by the memory of index cards. *Good morning, Gus* the white strip read. *Do you want to play a game?* The card was taped to the cupboard that Gus opened first thing each morning. "Mo-om!" he shouted, "Where're the Pop-Tarts?"

With carnival eyes, Jill appeared. "Read the message."

"Why?"

"It's a game, that's all. Find the Pop-Tarts. I've hidden little clues all over the house. All you have to do is read each one and they will lead you to the box. Doesn't that sound like fun?"

Gus turned his back on his mother and, over the scuffle of his retreating Scooby-Doo slippers, mumbled. "Never mind. I'm not really hungry."

Mother, may I?

By January, a recalcitrant fog had settled over the Oberdorf apartment. There was no escaping it. The Reading Chart was affixed to the fridge beneath a flimsy magnet that read: "A room without books is like a body without soul." Every time Gus opened or shut the refrigerator door, the laminated chart belly-flopped to the floor with an impudent slap.

Daily, hourly, those twenty mandatory minutes loomed. Jill had employed every strategy and timetable she could think of: before breakfast, first thing when they got home, with a snack, after a snack; no snack until you get it done, mister! Acid shot up like a red flag as the dinner hour approached and still the box that read *How Much Did We Read Today?* was empty. Gone were the evenings of downtime, of solace, of playing Fish. With heavy shoulders, Jill tried again: before cartoons, after cartoons, in the bath, in the bed, even after he was already asleep, the words like a lullaby she hoped might enter his psyche by osmosis.

With each passing day—each new campaign launched with promise and abandoned like a book that failed to spark the imagination—despair and hope wrestled like Old Testament angels in Jill's weary heart. She was a college English teacher for God sakes. She knew full well the consequences if she failed. This was the thought that haunted her each night as she kissed her son on the forehead, half-praying for a miracle. This was the thought that awoke with her at dawn as she poured, like a talisman, his favorite bowl of Lucky Charms, and waited.

One week shy of the winter grading period and Jill was tempted just to give up, give in, to spin her surrender as a loving act of acceptance of the clear and impervious truth that her son was not, nor would he ever be, a reader. Wearily, Jill unfolded her morning paper and fanned it as a shield as Gus pulled out his chair with a linoleum squawk.

"Can I have the Sports Section?"

A drop of melted butter clung to the corner of Jill's stunned mouth. Resisting the urge to say *may I*, she daubed her lips and slowly, gingerly, so as not to imperil any inchoate epiphanies, slid the requested section across the table. With slow, unobtrusive breaths, she watched her son trace his fingers along the enormous black headline type, colored marshmallow-tinted milk dripping from his small, decoding lips: SPRING TRAINING BEGINS TODAY! GOD BLESS AMERICA!

As if the red dirt kicked up from those mythic, faraway cleats had awakened something primordial in his seven-year-old body, Gus's arm began to twitch and toss. Fastballs and knuckleballs and imaginary splitters were hurled endlessly from his small, empty hand into the air. Body and mind suddenly converged mightily on a single path. By April, his nightly cartoons were replaced by Major League Baseball—

any team, anywhere—and in the morning, over Wheaties, a scrupulous analysis of the box scores. Twenty minutes, ha! Each morning at breakfast he devoured—if not in pace, then in spirit—the words of Plasche and Simmers and Sondheimer and Adante. "*Never before has a season so full of promise turned so quickly sour by the a-cra-mo-knee-us-*" Jill looked up over the editorial section and clarified. "Acrimonious means bitterly hateful." Gus repeated, "*—the a-cri-monious dugout of the league's most overpaid, overrated, aren't-we-all-just-over-them-by-now, team?*" Looking up brightly, Gus said. "There. Now can I play?" Jill reached over the top of his paper and tapped the next paragraph. Gus continued without a fight. "*If this is how they plan to behave, forget about it. I, for one, am in favor of dumping the whole lot of them for a few dozen, hardworking, baseball lovin' Little Leaguers.*" As if tryouts might already be underway, Gus leapt from his seat. "There, that's the whole paragraph. Now can I play?"

"May I."

"C'mon, mom. I've seen kids around school with team caps on already. You've got to call."

"One more paragraph."

"No."

"One more paragraph," she reasserted.

In the same willful staccato, he replied, "Not. Until. You. Call." From the pocket of his favorite jeans, Gus pulled out a creased scrap and handed it across the table. "I got the number off the bulletin board at school."

Jill smiled as Gus peeled her fingers from the coffee cup and replaced it with the phone. Compared to the warm mug, the receiver was cold and hard. Like rules. Like deadlines. All this time she'd been acting as if the day she finally gave Gus the nod they'd simply walk down the street and straight up to bat. Suddenly, that seemed naive. "Um, yes, hello," she said, nervously, "I'd like to inquire about enrolling my son for one of your baseball teams?"

Gus flapped his arms and whispered madly, "Say Little League."

Her fingers pressed to her free ear like a muffle, she turned inward; away. "Oh, I see. Back in January?"

Gus's arms fell limp. Jill had no way of knowing that, deep inside his burgeoning psyche, he was already comparing the sinking feeling in his heart to the movement of a major league change-up. She only knew that his eyes had begun to crimp and well. Gripping his wrist to keep him from fleeing, she pleaded, "Couldn't you make room for one more child?" Their eyes locked in mutual desperation. "He's not very big."

Jill was reminded, in the silence, of her own dogged refusal to leave the side of her parents' sealed caskets, as if, by sheer force of will or endurance, she could possibly change things. "No, I understand," she said.

Judging by the cataclysmic slam of his bedroom door, Gus did not.

The longest year of their lives.

That's when the thumping began. The undeniable sound of a Little League hard ball thrown against the wall that divided their bedrooms, threatening to bring down the building if some means of absorbing Gus's thwarted boy energy was not found, and quick. The solution came on aisle 43 of the Home Depot: a 4'x8' slab of plasterboard that Jill propped up against Gus's bedroom wall with a life-sized poster of Barry Bonds taped to the left side and a blue crayoned square for a strike zone. Thump! From May to September Gus sat with his ball and his new leather glove, his head cocked slightly as if attuned to nuance, as he studied the pros on TV. He grew two inches. He read four books. He started 2nd grade. His teacher was a man, Mr. Gallegos, who, because it was fall, tossed around a football with the children at recess. The World Series came and went, heralding the end of the season, but Gus's single-minded desire continued like a pulse. *Thump!* Paint dust flurried from the bare, nail-speckled space above Jill's desk; it was only a matter of time before the ball would begin to assert itself through the plaster like a face from a marble slab. THUMP! On a paper turkey he made out of the shape of his hand Gus wrote, I am thankful that there are only 47 more days until Little League sign-ups. For Christmas Jill gave him a real metal bat and an authentic Dodger jersey and a book on pitching tips by

Nolan Ryan. Gus read it straight through over the winter break and wrote a book report for extra credit. When Jill asked Mr. Gallegos how Gus was doing in reading, he looked genuinely confused. "Was there a problem?"

THUMP!!!

A hairline crack in the wall announced that it was time. Jill removed the yellow foam plugs from her ears and smiled. Gone were the 250 days of penance. The pouting, the waiting, the doubting, the regret, the heartache, the guilt, the head-pounding thumping, all gone as Jill stepped into the narrow hall and, tapping twice lightly, opened the door to Gus's room. He was seated on the edge of the bed, glove on hand, ball in glove, jersey that he'd slept in tucked into his new elastic waist baseball pants.

"Ready?"

As if The Call had just come into the bullpen, Gus tipped the visor of his cap and, with a reverent and wholly unironic nod, replied, "Ready."

Welcome to North Palms.

Sign-ups were from 9:00 to noon. At 8:37 a.m., in the faded blue mid-sized sedan she'd inherited from her parents fourteen years earlier and kept for reasons she could not fully articulate, Jill turned up the steep driveway that led to the fields of North Palms Little League. The parking lot was like a ghost town set. Jill scanned the abandoned fields as if whole teams of kids might suddenly jump out and yell *Surprise!*

"First ones here," she said brightly. Reaching over to pat his knee, she added, "I'd say that's a good sign."

Gus was already out the door, drawn toward the nearest field like a pilgrim to Mecca. There was nothing to look at, not even so much as a skitter of sprinkler for the eye to track. But there was something in the greenness. Something animate. As if the memory of every game that had ever been played and the promise of every game to come were somehow alive and pulsing in the chlorophyll. Even Jill could feel its pull.

Suddenly, there was a van beside her. A woman in a North Palms sweatshirt hopped out of the front seat, baseballs spilling out onto the asphalt at her feet. "Hey, there. Sorry to keep you waiting." She scooped them up like an errant juggler and said, "Just give me a sec to set up."

"We're a little early," Jill said, grabbing a stray ball. "We just wanted to make sure we got on a good team."

The woman's pink face broke out in a jack-o-lantern grin. "First timers, huh?" The back of her van looked like the locker room at Yankee Stadium. Hoisting a cardboard box off a pile of dirt-caked duffle bags, she finagled it onto one hip, and slammed the hatch. "C'mon."

At the far end of the lot, wedged between two of the three playing fields, was a squat, stucco building with a side door and a green painted, wood-flapped order window. "Just give me a minute here!" she grunted from inside. "I've just gotta—open—this—thing—" Her voice buckled under the strain of the hinged green panel. "—up. There we go." Securing the wood to a hook in the ceiling, she stepped down off the stool, flushed. "Now, first things first. Let's make sure you're in the right place. Did you bring a utility bill with you?"

"Oh, yes. Here's a phone bill. And here's a check for the registration. And here's Gus's birth certificate." Pointing to her son's birthday, she said proudly, "He's eight."

The baseball woman looked down at the line that read D.O.B. and grimaced. "Actually, he's nine."

Whatever Jill's shortcomings as a mother, knowing her son's age was not one of them. "My son is eight."

"Well, technically." The woman jotted something inscrutable on Gus's application. "But since he's going to turn nine before the end of the season, he's what we call League-age nine."

"But his birthday's in July. The lady on the phone told

27

me the season ended Memorial Day."

"Except for the all-stars. They go on through the middle of summer."

Jill's heart quickened as she considered the odds that someone had heard Gus practicing through the walls of their apartment; could tell just from his powerful and incessant thumping how good he would be. "You mean, they already want him for the all-stars?"

The baseball woman leaned in as if to leak good news to a friend. "I wouldn't get your hopes up. Most of these kids have been playing up here since they were five."

In the desert of her mind Jill could see them off in the distance, all the strapping becleated boys so far ahead and running further still. From some untapped abyss, tarry bubbles oozed up in Jill's throat and burst like bobbing fists: in that moment, there was nothing she wouldn't say or do to minimize that merciless divide. "Don't you worry about Gus. His dad's a professional baseball player."

"Really?" the woman said. With searchlight eyes she swooped down to the birth certificate.

Like a ripcord, Jill withdrew it. "You're done with this, right?" Sliding the paper back into her purse, she added, "Hate to lose these things."

The baseball woman smiled dubiously. "So, can we put him down for a little coaching, then?"

"What?"

"Your husband? You think he'll be able to make some time for the kids."

"Oh. No. Gus's dad and I are not together."

"That's okay. A lot of our out-of-the-home dads find it's a good way to get in some quality father/son time."

Jill turned to verify the location of her son who was still spot welded to the chain link fence. "Well, he travels a lot. As you can imagine." Sensing her story lacked the necessary details for credibility, Jill added, "They have to go play all those other teams and everything."

The baseball woman leaned in so close her lips kissed the dusty screen window. "Which team did you say he played for?"

Jill chose this moment to secure the snap on the top of her purse. "He's in negotiations right now, so, I'm not really at liberty to say."

"I see. Well, you'll let us know if he becomes available."

"Of course."

Licking the tips of her fingers with pursed lips, she loosened a flyer from the top of the stack. "Well, then, here's a list of our volunteer opportunities for you to look over. Tryouts will be in a couple of weeks."

"They have tryouts for eight-year olds?" Jill stood corrected. "I mean, nine-year olds?"

"It's just to make sure the teams are even, that's all. Just have his *dad*—" The baseball woman stretched the word out so it hung in the air twice as long as the others. "—take him over to the cages a few times. I'm sure he'll be fine."

A line was beginning to form behind her. Jill backed away as the baseball woman slid a clipboard under the slot for the next arrival. "Hey there, slugger. Welcome back!"

Jill may not have known much about Little League, but she knew what *even* meant. It meant there were kids people wanted and kids people didn't want. There were Tortoises and there were First-Round Draft Picks. A cunning glint suddenly flashed across Jill's brow. And then, she smiled, there were Ringers. With no particular gentleness, she tugged Gus free of the fence. "Let's go."

"Go where?" he asked, his eyes still floaty with visions of green.

"The cages."

"The batting cages?"

Grateful for the clarification, Jill said assuredly, "Of course, the batting cages."

Slammo.

The token machine at the batting cages spit Jill's dollar out like a fake i.d. She thumbed the wrinkled edges smooth and reinserted the bill three times before the tokens that would enable her only child to stand voluntarily before a hardball-spitting cannon appeared in the dish with a tinny clank. A man with skin like catgut shouted something incomprehensible in passing. Had it not been for the *Slammo* logo on his mangy cap, Jill would have taken him for a drunk who'd been sleeping one off in the scrub between the cage backs and the freeway. As it was, she figured he must be in charge. "Excuse me. Which one of these is the slowest?"

The man answered with a jerk of his head. "That one's 25."

"That's for softball, mom," Gus said.

"Well, maybe that's better to start with."

"It's for girls!! "

"That's not true, is it?"

The Slammo man flashed his sepia teeth and said, "Yeah, it pretty much is."

"I'm going in the 45," Gus said and, without waiting around for a no, grabbed a batting helmet from the rack.

With suspect eyes, Jill assessed the grungy headgear and the likelihood of public funk being transmitted through the crumbling foam liner. Her fears were momentarily assuaged by the thought of bowling shoes, and the certainty that here, too, some sort of antibacterial regulations must be in effect. She was on the verge of asking about them when the Slammo man hawked a loogie three inches from the drinking fountain. Ignorance was bliss she decided and turned to find Gus, helmet rakishly secured, standing on the step that led to the cage where the 45-mile-an-hour balls were thrown.

"Jesus H. Christ, Zach!" A man in thigh-hugging gym shorts was standing directly behind home plate and barking at a boy not much taller than Gus through the wire mesh. "That ball's been in the glove five minutes before you're moving on it!"

Jill took a seat on the bench several feet behind them. She watched her son's head turn toward the man's harsh voice, saw his soft gaze zero in on the coursing Adam's apple in the man's grizzled neck. Again, the son swung and missed. Gus turned his head toward the father and awaited his correction. "Whatya have, cement in those shoes? C'mon, let's see you step into it."

The final ball in the round was still en route when Zach pulled off his helmet and shoved open the cage door. Gus jumped back as the father shouted, "Get back in there, you need another round!"

"There's someone waiting, Dad."

Turning to the unattended boy, the man winked, "You

don't mind do ya, kid?"

In a single, lionesque move, Jill pounced, inserting herself in the space between them. "I'm sorry. Is there some confusion about whose turn it is?" Jill had not intended to stand so close. The man's slabbed chest suddenly blindsided her with a melee of stirrings: to pound on it, to spread her fingers across its curves, to see her son in its musky crook.

"No confusion. My kid's gonna take another turn, that's all. You keep batting till you're done— that's how it works here."

Jill's eyes traced the name embroidered across his v-neck wind shirt. Lifting her finger up past his sunburst nose, she pointed. "Well, Rod, the sign says otherwise."

Rod clenched his jaw beneath his Robocop sunglasses and taunted her in singsong. "The sign says otherwise." With a gruff swipe, he turned. "Alright, Zach, get out. Let's see what the momma's boy can do."

Jill gave Zach wide berth as she placed a token in Gus's hand. She waited for him to leap into position, to stare down the machine, to hit one straight through the back of the netting and out over the 405 Freeway—that'd show him—but found her son, instead, standing at the entrance, immobilized. "What is it?" Jill whispered.

With more eyes than words, Gus said, "Can you just do it?"

Rod's titanium sunglasses burnt a hole in Jill's

periphery. She stepped up to the door of the cage. "Do what?"

"Can you just put the token in?"

"Oh," Jill said. "Sure."

The mean eye of the pitching machine seemed to hold Gus in its bead. He dashed to safety on the other side of the batter's box, cueing his mother with a no sweat nod. Fighting the urge to duck and run herself, Jill slipped the token in the slot, stepped swiftly, but calmly, out of the cage and slammed the door tight.

The first ball spat out across the plate and rebounded with a dull boom against the backboard. "It's okay, buddy," Jill said. "You'll get the next one."

"Not standing like that he won't," Rod muttered. He was still standing in the prime viewing spot directly behind the batter.

"This is his first time here," Jill said. "So why don't you just give us a break." With a hippy and determined sidestep, she insinuated him off-center. "Do you mind?"

"Hey kid!" Rod shouted. A ball caromed off the back of Gus's helmet as he turned to the man's commanding voice. Rod smirked. "Rule number one. Don't ever take your eye off the ball."

Jill's hands flew up in the air. She was contemplating wrapping them around Rod's neck, when she saw Gus nod gratefully and return his keen gaze to the machine. "Now, bend your knees," Rod said.

And Gus obliged.

"Now choke up on the bat." Before Jill had a chance to claim ignorance on her son's behalf, Gus dutifully scooched his fingers up the barrel and swung; the ball shot off his bat like a missile. Jill glowed. Rod turned to his own son and knuckled him in the arm. "See, the momma's boy knows how to listen."

Zach refused to look up. "Can we just go already?"

"Hey, kid," Rod said, edging back to center stage. Jill gave an inch. "I'm going to yell swing, and you go. Show Zach how it's done."

What Gus knew had not been learned. The bend of his knees, the tilt of his torso, the juxtaposition of his bent wrist to his chin— every part of his body simultaneously coiled and loose. It was all strangely, unsettlingly, organic, as if the posture were already in him, like yeast in dough, and was now, under the finger scratch of Rod's voice, simply being revealed.

"Now!" he shouted. Before the "w" was off his fat, chapped lips, Gus had walloped the ball so hard it wedged itself in the netting in the upper right corner of the cage. In celebration, Rod swatted his son on the head. "Why can't you do it like that?"

Zach threw his batting gloves at his father's feet and ran off across the parking lot. Half expecting her to commiserate, Rod turned to Jill and shrugged, "Kids."

In Rod's absence the cage seemed suddenly rudderless. Jill reclaimed the center position as Gus proceeded to swing and miss. "That's okay, honey. You're doing really well." Jill admired how athletic he looked just standing there. As for why the ball was failing to hit the bat, this she couldn't say. At the next thud-and-whoosh, she squinted in an effort to deconstruct his motions, but it all happened too fast. It was, Jill hated to admit, much harder than analyzing a piece of prose; there, at least the words stood still while you mulled them over, but this: how anyone could see what was really going on was beyond her. Even more baffling was the fact that he was totally unable to duplicate something he'd just done perfectly two seconds before. Why wasn't it like walking or spelling or typing: once you'd mastered the motions you could do them effortlessly from there on in, only faster and better each time? Evidently this hitting of a ball with a stick was more complex. Desperate to contribute, Jill shouted, "Just choke on it, honey." But having no idea what she'd asked him to do, she couldn't say for sure whether he'd listened.

Who's your daddy?

Jill had planned to tell him once Gus was born. Once Gus started to walk. Said mama. Dada. Where's dada? By two, she no longer felt obligated to offer an explanation to anyone but her own son. "Your father wasn't ready for a family," she explained one night over Stegasaurus-shaped chicken bites and succotash. Fearing her explanation had been too pejorative, she quickly added, "He had big things to do." From that day on, any further inquiries were deflected with a mysterious wave and a vague I Already Told You, leaving Gus to conjure up fathers on Mars, on mountaintops, in top secret meetings with bulletproof attaché cases, or, if the speculation of his first-grade nemesis, Nevil Pratching, was to be believed, in an orange prison jumpsuit picking up trash on the side of the road.

The $64,000 Question

With only a week to go until tryouts, every free moment was used for review. Tracing the baselines in the fogged bathroom mirror Jill drilled him. "Okay, now, what do you call the person who stands between the second base and the third base?"

From behind the shower curtain, Gus replied, "The shortstop."

"Good." Jill X-ed a shortstop in the steamed glass. "And what is his job?"

"He fields the balls that go up the middle and then throws out whichever runner he can get."

"Are you sure?"

"Yes," Gus said. "We're out of shampoo."

Jill took out a new bottle from under the cabinet and pulled back the curtain where Gus sat soaking in a sudsy tub. He didn't move a modest muscle. He was only eight, after all (not nine!). Just an eight-year old boy, naked and unembarrassed. As if begging to differ, Gus pulled the plastic curtain shut. Jill stepped back, regrouped. "Okay," she said. "You've got three people in the outfield. What do you call the one who stands on the left side?"

Gus droned, "The left fielder."

"No."

"Yes."

Jill shook her head, and flip-flopped. "No, no. You're right. I was getting it mixed up with the theater. Stage left, stage right. Never mind. You've got it."

"Let's talk about the pitcher, mom."

"Oh, I don't think you're going to be pitching this first year. You know, the lady did say some of the other boys might be just a little bit more experienced than you."

"C'mon. Ask me something about pitching."

"What do pitchers like to eat for dinner?"

"Mo-om, c'mon. Seriously."

"Alright. One question. Then it's time to get out." Jill scanned the grout line for inspiration. "What do you call the dirt he stands on?'

"The mound. C'mon, something harder."

Jill wiped the steamed mirror clear with her shirtsleeve and said, "I don't know anything harder."

"Okay," Gus said, "Then, I have one for you. What's the most strikeouts a major league pitcher ever got in a game?"

Jill frowned. "How many batters are there, again?"

"Nine."

"Okay, well, let's see, there're nine players, and it seems like they each get a couple of turns—

"At bats," Gus corrected.

"So, I'm going to say twelve."

Gus aped a buzzer. "Wrong. Twenty. Roger Clemens

did it twice. Randy Johnson and Carry Woods did it once. Okay, next question..."

"One more, then it's time to get out."

"Which pitcher has the most wins in the major leagues?"

"I don't know. Hank Aaron?"

"Mom, Hank Aaron was an outfielder."

"Good to know. All right, buddy," she said, snapping the towel from the rack, "If your fingertips get any prunier you won't be able to pitch at all."

"C'mon, mom. Just one, more. Pleaasse.... "

Jill's decision-making process always followed the same circular logic. If Gus's father were here he would play this game with Gus till his skin fell off, but— "All right. One more. But I mean it this time, Gussy. One."

"Okay. This is going to be a tough one."

"Why?" Jill smiled. "Because I did so well on the others?"

"Tell me the difference between a knuckleball and a slider."

"Oh. Wait." Jill's lips parted and froze, as if trying to restrain a thought. "I know this one." The words crawled up out the crust of her cerebellum like possums from a deep sleep. In the same slow, certain manner in which she used to unfurl the letters that led her to many a school spelling bee championship, Jill explained, "A knuckleball is slow, and flutters like a butterfly. And a slider is a medium fastball that curves."

The sound of the curtain rings sliding back was like a jaw dropping. "How'd you know that?"

Jill buried her mouth in the warm, blue terry cloth and, through muffled lips, said, "I don't know. Just one of those dumb trivia things you pick up in college."

Tryouts.

The judges were positioned in the outfield by fiefdom. An inner sanctum of advisors—assistants, drinking buddies, fathers of star players—flanked each of the six minor league managers, who sat imperiously in sagging lawn chairs. Armed with their clipboards and the power of the gods, they made their stealth notes and shot their arch glances and mercilessly whispered behind the trembling backs of the children. Even from a hundred feet away, Jill could tell that the one seated smack dab in center field, the one with the bullhorn and the widest berth, was Rod.

There were boys everywhere. Tall boys, short boys, wiry boys, blubbery boys, boys who, even at eight or nine, already bore the markings of bullies, and boys who, even at eight or nine, were certain to be the ones who those bullies would hang up by their belt loops in the middle school bathroom. Usually Jill could tell everything she needed to know about a boy by looking him in the eye and finding there the telltale signs of acumen, decency, self-restraint, but this was a different playing field. Here, a boy's face was all but concealed by the shade of his cap. Here, the only thing that mattered was his body and what he could do with it, and whether Gus could do it better or worse. The desire to mentally eliminate the competition was as natural as incisors on baby back ribs; already Jill found herself being grateful for the runts, and how they impacted the curve.

"Go get 'em," she said as Gus's group was called to the outfield and lined up along the back fence. One by one, the boys were called up to demonstrate their skills: fielding, throwing, hitting, running. They started in the shortstop position. Balls were hit in their direction, low ones mostly, ones they were expected to catch and throw to an older boy who was standing on first base. Ball one went straight through the spindly legs of the first boy, who, Jill noted with something perversely like pleasure, was several inches shorter than Gus.

"Get your glove on the ground, okay. Let's try again." The gentle voice came from the man who was hitting the balls from behind home plate. He was slim and soft-shouldered with wire rim glasses. "Ready?" With an encouraging nod, he sent ball two straight down the middle. The small boy got just enough glove on it to tip it away. He scrambled to recover, then, as if planning on delivering the ball in person, ran halfway to first base before throwing it. "Way to stay with it, nice job."

Jill inclined her ear to the gentle man's voice. Clearly he was not like those other men, the ones in the outfield, the Roddish ones. He was decent, caring, no doubt well read.

From across the field the bullhorn sounded and, from Rod's snide lips, the words, "Next up. Gus Oberdorf."

The Nice Coach called out, "Ready, Gus?"

Gus nodded and took the ready position: legs spread, knees bent, glove out and open wide just above the dirt. The test grounder shot off the bat. Jill traced the path of the ball like a golfer's putt headed straight for Gus's mitt. All her worry had been for nothing. Her son could hold his own against the best of them. He could make this play and then some; make the whole brawny, clipboarded cabal shake their thick skulls and wonder where this Gus Oberdorf had been hiding. A foot from the mouth of his deftly-positioned glove, and the ball suddenly shot up like a hiccup—like a cruel shove in front of an oncoming train—leaping inexplicably over Gus's shoulder and clear out to the dead fringe of grass in left field. Jill's hand flew up to her mouth as if to hold something back: consolation, expletives, vomit.

"Bad hop, buddy," the Nice Coach said. "Let's try another one."

Jill needed answers and the nearest neutral body that could provide them. Standing apart from the parented bleachers, in the shade of a misplaced pine, was an old man so stoop shouldered and leather faced he seemed to predate the game. "Excuse me," Jill said. "But what does that mean, bad hop?"

The man shot a plume of smoke from the side of his mouth and, with a glint that still held the blue of summer skies, said, "Did you see the ball?"

"Yes," she said with a studious nod.

"That's a bad hop."

Jill wanted to ask him if the bad part of the hop would somehow go down on Gus's permanent record, but there was no time: the second ball was already racing across the mound.

Gus scooped it straight up and threw it to the first baseman's glove. He made it look so easy, too easy. "That was good, right?"

The old man, whose satin baseball jacket bore the markings of many long-forgotten championships, said, "Got the runner. Can't ask for more than that."

Jill didn't actually see a runner; wondered if, in fact, dying coaches kept their dreams alive with imaginary friends. "You mean, in theory, right?"

The old man responded with a look that said nothing had been right in the world since they started letting women hang out at the ballpark. Turning away from the sting, Jill saw the third ball: a high line drive. Gus's arm shot up like a lizard's tongue and snagged it. She could hear the smack of the ball against her son's leathered hand. Flushed and beaming, she turned to the old man to extend the afterglow. "He's never even played before."

The old man sucked the air from a gap in his back tooth. "That's just reflexes. You either got 'em or you ain't."

Whatever crusty charm Jill had found in him earlier was gone. She needed to know that Gus had done well, (or at least not badly). She needed to know that he was good (or at least not horrible). The need for reassurance was so palpable it propelled her straight to the fence behind home plate. "So, what do you think? Did he do okay?"

The Nice Coach turned back and smiled. "He did great."

"He's never even played before."

"Don't worry. He'll do fine."

The downgrade from great to fine triggered a new flurry of despair. "So, do you think you'll pick him?"

"Even if I wanted to, there's no guarantee I'd get him."

From across the field, the bullhorn sounded. "Next up, Linus Macaw."

"But you'd like to pick him, right?"

"Don't worry. Whoever gets him will be lucky to have him."

Jill pressed her lips up to the fence and, with more guttural breath than was appropriate, said, "But I want you."

The Nice Coach held up a flat palm to the outfield and met Jill at the fence. "You know I'm the coach for the Minor Tigers, right?"

"The name's not important."

"But you know we came in last last year?"

Jill paused for a moment to process the information. "Doesn't that mean you get first pick?"

The bullhorn answered her from across the field. "Would the nervous mom by the fence please sit down."

Ripples of laughter spread out through the crowd as the fretful parents seized the opportunity for comic relief.

Jill backed away as if from a deported lover. "His name is Gus—"

"Gus Oberdorf," he said, and then added the two cryptic words that would torment her for the rest of the week. "I remember."

Jill was almost entirely sure that's what he had said. But as she replayed the words in her head, retraced the arc and ebb of his lips as he'd spoken, she was forced to consider the possibility that what he had actually said was not *I* but *I'll*. Never had an apostrophe double ell been more critical. *I remember* meant that Gus had made such an impression that anyone would remember his name, that all the coaches would want him, that he could just as easily end up with Rod. *I'll remember* was a promise, a vow to take the name Gus Oberdorf into the draft and shout it out first chance he got because, deep down where these negotiations are really made, the Nice Coach intuited that Jill and Gus were like him, intellectual souls in a brute world, and they would, understandably, have to stick together.

Or maybe, Jill sighed as she attempted to reclaim her spot on the bleachers and discovered it taken, *I remember* simply meant that the Nice Coach, the undoubtedly well-read coach, was good with names; nothing more.

Cup shopping.

Jill was unnerved to discover that it was nothing like shopping for bras. There was no designated department. There were no helpful size charts or swooping sales women who had the exact same one at home in three colors. There was just a pegboard panel with hooks on a wall in a row with the shin guards and the mouth guards and the masks that covered entire young faces. And this was not about anything as frivolous as sagging. Grandchildren were at stake.

"Excuse me," Jill said. Gus instinctively drifted off toward the bat display as a carbuncle-cheeked sales boy answered Jill's call. "Maybe you can help me."

Jill held two cups up to the clerk's reddening nose. "This one here says Youth Small, which is a size six to eight. And this one here is a Youth Medium, which is a ten to twelve. So what do you usually recommend for an eight going on nine-year-old?"

The teenager eyed Gus's hiding place by the bat rack enviously. "I really couldn't say, ma'am. Would you like me to get the manager?"

"Yes. Why don't you do that." Turning to position Gus in her eye line, she held each cup up in its imaginary position, one, then the other, like a cameraman plotting his shot.

A man with a dated mustache rounded the corner. "I'm

the manager. May I help you?"

"I just need some advice on these cups." Up and down the neighboring aisles, boys scattered like delinquents. "I'm concerned that this one might be too small, but this one," she said, holding it up to the light and rolling her eyes, "Looks way too big, don't you think?"

The manager looked over at Gus who shoved his hands in his pockets and whisper shouted, "Can't we just get both of them?"

"That's probably best," the manager offered quickly.

"Are they returnable?"

"I'm afraid not."

"Well, I'm not going to spend $9.99 on a cup you're never going to use. That's just a waste." Turning back to the manager she said, "Isn't there some way you could help size him for me?"

The man smiled so tightly his mustache brushed his jaw line. "Not really, no."

He'd left her no choice. Squatting down, Jill held each cup up to Gus's zipper line.

"Mo-om!!"

"If you want to play baseball you need a cup that fits. That's all there is to it. I'm sure Ronald Clemens's mom had to do this when he first started, too."

"Roger," Gus corrected.

"Roger," Jill said, then stood up with a resigned sigh.

"Well, I'm not sure either of them is perfect, but, I say the safe bet is the big one. You can always grow into it." She tilted it on its side and squinted, as if measuring flour in its capacious hollow.

Gus's eyes widened at the prospect of the vast, demanding shell. Unable to articulate the particular threat of the larger cup, he merely shook his head and, raising his index finger up like E.T.'s, pointed to the smaller one.

Opening day.

Jill had thought that Norman Rockwell's America had died off with her own suburban childhood or, more likely, had never existed at all— was merely an irresistible hallucination sustained by the nation's collective imaginations. Yet here it was in all its hot dog-grilling glory, resurrected on an unlikely hilltop in the center of a city known more for silicone and gangs and high-end divorces than flag-waving; but wave it did, high up on a rusting pole surrounded at the base by a cheery circle of newly-planted petunias. A woman in a calico apron leaned out from the snack bar window and shooed away three carelessly darting boys. "Get away from those flowers!"

It was a riot of color and noise and baseball dreams, boys swaggering loudly in their new plastic cleats, girls strutting sassily in their new softball scrunchies, babies—future all-stars every one—shaded in strollers along the outside of the fence where parents were lined up three deep, jostling for camera angles. All around the perimeter of the field the kids were clustered by team, by division, the t-ballers giddy and squirming, the seniors skulking along the back fence too cool for pomp but, nonetheless prepared to march out and take their places in the great American pastime.

A jury-rigged P.A. spat out fragments of inaudible announcements...*thanks to all the...new sod ... don't the bleachers look ... we have a lost toddler by the ... pancake breakfast tickets ... let's pitch in with trash... umpires are just volunteers, so...please, no dogs.* A zaftig teen in a gold lame gown teetered out to the mound for a uniquely-keyed version of *God Bless America.* The Boy Scouts paraded out next, followed by a man from the NCAA whose job it was to indoctrinate the children with the message that the reason to play sports was—repeat after me—"Playing sports is fun!" and that the odds that any one of them would go on to merit a college athletic scholarship was one in five-hundred thousand. Around the fence, several fathers nodded in acknowledgment of how hard that information must have been for the other dads to hear. Two fire engines sparked a minor panic until it was decided, as if in one communal sigh, that they were part of the fanfare. All-star teams from the year before were called up to stand with their banners, while resolutions were made for new kids—our kids, my kid—to be standing up there in the year to come. And finally, as the line for the first french fries of the season began to mount, the long-haired pastor from the equipment manager's church blessed the season in a lengthy— and, according to the four people standing close enough to hear him, humorous—invocation.

All of Jill's hard work had paid off: Gus was now a minor Tiger. She could not conceive of a better team, a nicer coach, a more winning group of boys. Their uniforms were navy jerseys with white pants and orange striped socks to match the tiger logo on their shirt. Gus was neither the biggest nor the smallest: he was just right. He was perfect. They all were. The Minor Tigers. THE MINOR TIGERS!

Panning the rows of the other five minor teams, it was obvious that the minor Tigers were the most exemplary. Clearly, like attracted like. The minor Pirates had a shifty look about them. The minor Cardinals, with their red shirts and their little gold birdies, seemed a tad fey. Jill didn't quite have a handle yet on the Dodgers, although their blue and white uniforms appeared brighter than the other teams, so bright and crisp, in fact Jill could not help but wonder if the person in charge of the uniforms was related to the coach. The minor Braves had two boys the size of most twelve-year-olds. "Do those boys look a little old to you? " Jill mentioned casually to the mother beside her—a lovely woman, a Tiger mom—who furrowed and swatted her husband who in turn marched off toward the announcer's table to investigate. And then there was Rod's team, the minor Yankees. With their ridiculous black paint smears, they all looked like hooligans. Jill would rather her son not play at all than end up with a group like that.

"Would you all please.......your caps for the........Allegiance," the P.A. croaked. A hush fell upon the crowd as they followed the bright, sweet voice of some unseen girl who led them:

> *I pledge allegiance*
> *to the flag*

of the United States

of America—

The younger children placed their hands over their hearts lickety-split and held them there firmly. A shoulder's width in front of Jill, a man with a braided ponytail and a tank top and a tattoo of the U.S.S. Truman on his fleshy arm followed suit. Jill was slower to respond. A life spent in the company of academics had stunted her ability to go along with the crowd and whatever small joy might come from it. But the sight of Gus with his Tigers cap over his heart broke her; the sight of his resolute eyes dutifully raised and, in the warm, bar-be-cue-scented air, the sound of the name of the country of her birth uttered by a thousand strangers bound together by little more than the shared belief that their children could grow up to be President. Or better yet, Derek Jeter.

T-I-G-E-R-S!

Only the teams that had met in the championship games the year before played on Opening Day. That left the minor Tigers free for a meeting under a magnolia tree in the far corner of the parking lot. Bev, the team mom, brought a tub of Red Vines and placed it in the center of the circle, where the kids and Ned, the Nice Coach, sat cross-legged. Their parents stood in a ring behind them, as if a bonding round of Duck, Duck, Goose might be imminent.

"The Tigers are a team," Ned said, and the half-dozen boys who had been with him the year before let out a ferocious growl. "We practice like a team, we play like a team, we win like a team, and we lose like a team." The kids were not as enthusiastic about the last part. "C'mon guys, there's nothing wrong with losing as long as we tried our best. So let's hear it." The twelve boys whose destiny it was to be minor Tigers let out an encouraging roar. "Tigers! Tigers! GO0000000 Tigers!" All twelve of the boys and even some of their fathers growled.

Ned went on to explain that every Tiger played every position, that there were no regular starters, no Tiger stars. "Anyone who wants to pitch can pitch," he said. Gus whipped his head around to make sure that Jill had heard. "No one will get more at bats than anyone else. No one will get more turns in the infield than anyone else. And everyone will have the same amount of innings on the bench. Deal?"

Jill had not felt so pleased with herself since earning an honorable mention in the Great Western States short fiction competition. Gus could have been stuck with Rod or that shifty Pirates coach, but here he was on a team that would let Gus pitch, let Gus start, let Gus play every position. Maybe her slight delay in getting him into the sport had been for a reason. She was tempted to reconsider the existence of destiny, but having already denounced the entire concept based on the spectacularly obvious and axiomatic truth there could be no Meant To Be without a One Who Meant It—a possibility that had been eliminated entirely in her first quarter of freshman biology—any efforts to reclaim it now felt like chucking a platinum lighter for the lark of rubbing sticks. Dumb luck was what it was. Glorious dumb luck and a little motherly determination, and for that, Jill lifted her eyes up to the trellis of white, mitt-sized blossoms, and smiled gratefully.

No Tiger left behind.

A survey was taken to determine the most convenient days for the Tigers to practice. Jill said Mondays and Wednesdays were impossible. She had late afternoon classes on Monday and Wednesday. Any days but Monday and Wednesday would be fine. Ned counted up the show of hands and said, "Monday and Wednesday it is."

That night while Jill and Gus were down in the laundry room Bev, the team mom, called. According to the message, she was more than happy to pick Gus up from school and give him a snack and take him to practice and bring him home twice a week for the next four months, and Jill was not to feel guilty in the least because, in the end, they were all just Tigers. "And Tigers always stick—" The message was cut off mid-sentence. Jill assumed the missing word was "together" but she couldn't be entirely sure.

Shattered.

On the day of Gus's very first game, the North Palms parking lot was nearly filled to capacity. Jill slowed past the last row of vans and trucks and SUVs—hers, it seemed, was the only mid-sized sedan left in child-rearing America—until she spotted it. Right up front, along the low outfield fence where the major boys were warming up: four great big spots right in a row.

"Presidential!" Jill proclaimed, and gave Gus's knee a victorious pat. Gus stuffed the last half of his Rice Krispies treat in his mouth and handed his mother the wrapper.

"I'll be there before kickoff," Jill teased.

Gus rolled his eyes and leapt from the car, his bright orange socks showcased, old-school style, as he ran across the pavement to the adjacent field where the minors played. Jill had planned to spend the warm-up time grading papers, but the tedious and likely plagiarized examples of lunar imagery in *A Midsummer Night's Dream* could not compete with the major outfielders bounding like bomb-blasted soldiers just outside her picture window. Six feet in the air in all directions they dove. Nothing escaped their well-worn gloves. At twelve-years old some of them almost looked like men. How a boy who still needed help with his belt buckle was expected to turn into this in three short years required more imagination than even Jill possessed.

Everything was happening too fast: the pace of the game, the growth of her son, the speed of the hardball heading straight for her windshield. With a death thud, it struck. Lightning and hoarfrost shot straight through her bones as the safety glass spread out from the point of brokenness. Like shattered ice it spread, bit by mosaic bit, blue-white and weakening until the moment gravity and physics defied the fractured surface to bear the weight. She could see them plunging. As the ball fell through the hammock of glass, she could see her mother's long brown hair floating skyward in the frigid water. Her father's lips parted as if in a half-smile. The blinking red lights of the yellow bus vanishing beneath the unforgiving ice. On the floor of the car in which she last saw her parents alive, the baseball came to rest, death and life and the shards of each spilt at her feet like jigsaw puzzle pieces as she leapt trembling from the old sedan.

The Tiger bleachers.

By the time the league president and Jill's insurance company and the windshield repair service had been contacted, it was almost game time. On the tiered benches where Jill expected to find a familiar face, she found instead a crude burlesque. Interspersed between the moms and the dads and the grandmas and the grandpas and the assorted Sour Patch-chomping siblings was a recurring orange and black-striped cartoon face.

"Here you go," Bev said, hurtling three rows to hand Jill her Tiger-on-a-stick. "Whenever I say 'How 'bout those Tigers?' You hold this up and say, 'They're Greee-aaaat!' Okay?"

Jill studied the cereal box icon stapled to what appeared to be paint stirrers. "Where'd you get these?"

"I made them," Bev beamed. "Just bought a case of Frosted Flakes and cut the pictures right out. I got Lester's Paint & Lumber to donate the sticks. Will you be needing more than one?"

Jill was spared a response by the sight of the blue and orange and white-clad bodies streaming out onto the field. In a zealous burst, Bev leapt to her feet and began to fan her ample arms, a gesture of Tiger solidarity that obstructed the view. Jill craned her head in an attempt to identify the players. The first

60

baseman was too fat, the shortstop too brown, the third baseman too tall, the catcher too thick—

"Oh, look!" Beatrix said, her English accent as thick as scones. According to the Tiger phone list, she was the only other single mom on the team. "There's Ian. Out in that big grassy part over there."

Jill stared at the small boy with the oversized glove on his head, arms spinning like propellers, and said politely, "He looks very relaxed."

From center field, Jill scanned left, then right. It seemed likely they might need a player like Gus out there to cover for a boy with a mitt on his head, but judging from their ankle-length pant cuffs neither of the other outfielders was her son. With a magnanimous Tiger sigh Jill acknowledged that Gus would not actually be starting the game. She was fine with that. There were no Tiger starters she reminded herself, although she was quite certain the three boys sitting on the bench at this moment would beg to differ.

"How 'bout those Tigers?!" Bev shouted.

Jill lifted up her Tiger stick and shook it three begrudging times. It was only when Bev sat down that the mound and the boy who appeared to be walking its way came into view. There was no mistaking the orange socks, the brown ringlets curling up from under the edge of his cap. Watching her son trot diagonally across the field, she found herself praying he was en route to the first baseman, perhaps to deliver a message from the coach or, better yet, to take his place. First base would be fine, first base would be good—all you really had to do was stand there and open your glove—but seeing him stop at the center point of the game, she realized with a cold and heaving dread, that the mound was Gus's final destination.

"Isn't that your boy?" Beatrix chirped. "It looks like he's going to be the ringleader."

The air around her grew torpid and grainy. Gus was supposed to have his chance, sure, just like all the other worthy Tigers. But he wasn't supposed to start. He wasn't supposed to throw the first pitch of the first game of his first season ever. He wasn't supposed to be the bloody ringleader of the whole minor Tigers! The sense memory of shattering glass fed her distress. This was not like taking the training wheels off his bike and watching him disappear down the street, a private right of passage. It was not like the fazing out of morning good-byes from classroom door to school gate to idling car, a common and universal act of weaning. It was not even like the time Gus got stuck at the top of the ferris wheel all alone for nearly half an hour, his rickety bucket swinging precariously over the sea while Jill shouted up "stop kicking," knowing all the while that nothing she did or said would make the least bit of difference, that the whole slipshod contraption could come crashing down at her feet and there was not a book in the world that would help any of them understand it. No, this was different. This was prophetic. Chapter One, Verse One of her son's life's story, her role in which was to sit idly by, powerless to wipe a tear or a brow or the runs from the slate of a regrettable inning, a handcuffed witness to the great unknown. Jill wanted to disappear, to rise up in the air in her own rickety bucket and wage her private battle with nausea and terror and the urge to shout down to the metaphoric passersby *He's never even played before!!*

"Excuse me," she said, and fleeing to a nearby patch of dirt, found suitable solitude for the gnashing of teeth.

Play ball!

The first batter for the minor Dodgers stepped into the box in his bright blue and white uniform. Gus dug his cleat into the rubber as if he'd been doing it for years and threw the first pitch straight down the center and into the catcher's gloved hand.

"Steee--rike!"

A jolt of pure ecstasy spread out from the back of Jill's clenched throat, across her forehead, over her hips, and down through the place of his birth. She wanted to stop time, to bask in the joy of hearing that atavistic grunt declare her son's efforts valiant, but the game raced thoughtlessly on. Rocking back, Gus readied himself for pitch number two. The Dodger swung. And the Dodger missed.

"Stee-rike Two!"

Whatever happened next could never erase the fact that Gus had thrown two strikes. Two strikes in a row on his very first outing. Jill almost dared to turn her head towards the bleachers and the appreciative glow of the other Tiger parents, but decided it was better to wait for the final thrown strike. The first out of the game. As if from the inner chamber of an old Remington, a capital K rose up and—thwack!—imbedded itself in her mind's eye. Gus lifted his leg. He seemed to plant his foot even deeper, to thrust his arm up and out from a place even lower down in the scapula. And then, in the air space where she awaited the sound of Strike Three, it came. The dull blat! The blat and the yelp and the blurred blue jersey collapsing on the ground, and the sound of a hundred fans (well, maybe not quite a hundred) all gasping at the consequences of her son's one errant throw. This was the difference between writing and pitching. In writing, effort conspired towards progress. On the mound, nothing accrued. Pitches could not be rethought or revised or deleted. Two strikes without a third might as well have been a blank page.

The parents cheered sympathetically as the felled Dodger brushed off his pants and took his place on first base. Timidly, Gus threw a ball to the next batter. Then another. Then a third, each one further from the batter than the last. "C'mon, catcher," the Old Man shouted, "Give him a target."

The thought that the onus might be on someone other than her son drifted past like a blessing on the Old Man's smoke. Jill slowly sidestepped her way in his direction, inhaling as Gus entered his wind-up, exhaling as the ball threaded the strike zone, unhit. Twice. "The count is full!" the umpire shouted.

"Now we'll see what he's got," the Old Man said.

Jill leaned in so close she could feel the dusty warmth from his old nylon jacket as the ball crossed directly over the plate. Or at least according to anyone in attendance with 20/20 vision.

"Ball four. Take your base."

"Oh my God," Jill wailed, "That was straight over the plate!"

The Old Man clucked and flicked his spent butt in the dirt. "Sometimes you get the call. Sometimes the call gets you."

Withdrawing the pack of Pall-Malls from his pocket, he tamped one in her direction. Jill lifted her shoulders like a freshman at a high school prom and said, for the record, "I don't really smoke."

Brother, can you spare an out?

On the heels of the Great Injustice, Gus walked the next batter—or as Jill preferred to say, the next batter walked—and now, despite how well he was doing, the bases were somehow loaded. Nearly ten smoke-free years, and still she managed to suck hard enough to burn the paper halfway down the butt on the first drag. The fourth Dodger came to bat. In cool, short order, Gus threw two perfect strikes. Seven pitched strikes in all and still not an out to show for it. The bases were still loaded, the batters still threatening one after another to bring them all home; Gus was still out there all alone doing practically everything right. (What kind of sadist invented this game anyhow?)

Jill eyed her son for hairline cracks as he readied himself for the third pitch. It was all a blur. The release of the ball, the wallop of the bat, and now, a pop fly soaring high and far and deep into center field where Beatrix's son, Ian, was, as this moment, sitting down amidst his pluckings of grass and weeds. Shouts of "Get up!!" seemed to fall on deaf ears. As the hurtling ball began its descent, the voices shifted to cries of "Heads!!!"

Beatrix ran to the fence. "Cover your bloody bob, Ian!!"

Perhaps it was the sound of his mother's voice, or the whistle of the plummeting ball but, just like that, the boy looked up, somewhat startled it seemed, to find there was a game going on and that he was, in fact, in it. Noting the arc of the ball he closed his eyes and, with milliseconds to spare, stuck out his glove. The breath of a thousand spectators (all right, maybe it was a hundred) held still as the ball nicked the tip of the stiff, leather fingers and ricocheted off toward the outfield fence. A passel of Tigers converged upon it like a loose dollar in the wind while, in carefree succession, four Dodgers crossed home plate.

Beatrix turned from the fence and blew air through her frosted bangs. "Phew, that was a close one."

The Tiger parents were unsure of how to respond, all but Bev, who jumped back up in front of the bleachers and, lifting her cheer stick, cried, "Ian, Ian, he's our man, if he can't do it nobody can!"

Jill was tempted to remind the blathering fans that they still had NO OUTS, but fearing it would somehow reflect badly on Gus, she held her tongue, numbing it with the smoke of a second bummed butt.

Freshman Comp 101.

The good news was that the Dodger pitchers were even less consistent than Gus. After the twenty-six run tie was called on account of darkness, twenty-four little boys clamored out of their respective dugouts claiming victory and starvation, happy as spaniels. For Jill, the experience of those two-and-a-half excruciating hours had not been so easy to shake. Like a hangover it lingered, on through the night and into the next day, when the prospect of corrective measures—of proactive steps to ensure she would never have to suffer like that again— slid into an empty seat nearest the door. Jill eyed his broad shoulders. The tight expanse of t-shirt across his chest. On the first day of the semester she had dismissed him as an athlete, and nothing he had said or done since had prompted her to rethink her first impression. But that night, after Gus's debut game, Jill found herself reading his essay with new eyes, the way a mother might, as if each fleck of light beheld full moons of acuity. Handing back his paper she asked to speak with him after class, feeling keenly and unsettlingly aware, as she headed back up the aisle, of her sedentary, thirty-two-year-old posterior.

"I'd like to caution you about relying too heavily on colloquialisms," she said when the room had cleared. She was at her desk now, seated.

"Uh-hun," he said.

"It's important for you to commit to one voice—first or second person, formal or informal—whichever you choose is fine, but you need to be consistent."

"Consistent," he repeated. "Right."

"I just feel as if your writing has real potential, that's all—"

"Thanks." Even as his eyes stayed locked on hers, she could feel his body twisting toward the door. "Is that it?"

In search of nothing, Jill opened her desk drawer. "You're on the baseball team, right?"

The athlete nodded. "We're 6-and-1 this season."

Jill smiled. "The reason I wanted to talk to you is that my son just started playing Little League. He pitched his first game last night." She left a slight pause for him to be impressed, or at least interested, before continuing. "And, well, as you know, that can be a lot of pressure. So, I guess, I was just wondering if—"

"We've got a game here on Friday. Maybe you should bring him. I'm starting. My ERA's 2.36 right now. I'm trying to get it under two but I'm 1-and-0 for wins."

Why was she not surprised that he would answer her with stats? "Wow."

"Last week I struck out twelve guys," he added. "That's a record."

Pleased to have the opportunity to show off, Jill said, "I

thought the record was twenty. Robert Clemens, I think it was."

The ballplayer's bright, blue eyes dimmed. "Roger Clemens is in the majors. I just meant for colleges." His lids drooped further still. "Community colleges."

"Oh, well," Jill said, quickly trying to shore him back up, "That's still very impressive."

A girl with a twelve-inch gap between the top of her jeans and the bottom of her cropped top popped her head in the door. Her belly was as flat and brown as a well-groomed baseline.

With a jut of his firm chin, the pitcher instructed her to wait outside. "Yeah, so," he said to Jill. "Why don't you bring him to the game. Your son. So he can watch me. You can learn a lot by watching."

Feeling the heat off the bronzed skin of the girl, who was, despite her boyfriend's instructions, still leaning in the doorway— Jill's doorway—Jill prolonged the conversation.

"This Friday?"

"Yeah, seven o'clock," he said, adjusting his backpack.

"Do we just get the tickets there, or do we need to get them ahead of time?"

"I don't really know. Listen, I've gotta go."

"Eager to get started on next week's paper, right?" The pitcher looked at her in a way that made her feel unhinged; or seventy. "Joke," she said.

"Ah. Okay, well, thanks again for the A."

Jill lifted her hand in the air as if to wave something away—the implication, the memory, the peach-scented oil wafting in off the girl whose face disappeared in the baseball player's considerable chest before Jill could even get the words out. "You earned it."

The making of Gus.

The blank page had been glaring at her. That's how it all began. Paper, contrary to Anne Frank's assertion, was not proving itself to be patient at all: it was a snide and indefatigable taskmaster. Jill needed air. Air was good. Air stirred the senses, coaxed filaments of thought from the crannies and caves. A quick walk around the campus and characters would begin to whisper in her ear. Themes would form themselves into orderly plot points like coins in an automated sorter. Racing down the stairs—ha!—she threw open the doors of the Manzanita dorm. With her MA from the University of Arizona completed and a teaching job lined up in L.A. in the fall, a chance to stay on as resident advisor meant six carefree, rent-free months to do nothing but sleep and read and write.

She could see the lights on the field from two blocks away. There were no marching bands, just the pulsing hum of a crowd and a periodic voice broadcasting indecipherable names into the star-kissed night. The hum fell to a hush. She had the sense that the distant crowd was holding its breath. Jill quickened her pace as the mob exploded into a huzzah of visceral delight. She was nearly running now. Whatever it was that had made all those people so happy, she hoped it would happen again. Prepared for epiphanies and glorious distractions, she found instead a ticket window.

"That'll be five dollars."

Jamming her hands in her pockets, Jill came up with a napkin scrap. She unfolded it to find a forgotten scrawl of inspiration: *Is there a character named Gus?*

"Sorry. I forgot my wallet."

Jill backed away into the milling crowd. Startled by the reminder that she was actually out in the world and visible, she took stock of her clothes. Fashion was an afterthought.

Some days she'd find she'd stepped straight out of the daydreamy steam of her morning shower and into real life with no recollection of the brushing of teeth and the combing of hair and the selecting of the day's attire. Tonight, it was a sleeveless black t-shirt and jeans, a combination she had, over the years, come to understand she looked attractive in. With tentative fingers, Jill touched her hair. It was new. A woman with a master's degree needed more than a haphazard ponytail. The blunt-edged bob with bangs was intended to ground her in the outer world, to draw her eyes, like thick strokes of kohl liner, toward the here and now.

The field appeared in chinks and glimmers through the gaps in the stadium fence. As if guided by sonar, Jill sidestepped her way past the backs of the packed crowd. Beyond the seats there would be a clearing. She had never seen it—could not have said with any certainty that a baseball field even existed on the campus she'd inhabited for the past seven years; still, she drifted determinedly, past the banner that declared this the home of the U of A Wildcats, past the far end of the enclosure where the paying customers sat and cheered, towards the place where the obstacles narrowed. Just as she knew they would.

Now there was only a fence separating Jill from the big grassy area where three men stood fairly evenly spaced. The one closest to her suddenly crouched down. Jill studied the line of his roped calf, his clubbed forearm, his laser-gaze, until, without warning or provocation—at least none that Jill saw— he starting running straight towards her like a man from a wielded knife. Reflexively she leapt back, oblivious to the foul ball that dropped from the sky six inches from her head.

"That's not really a great place to stand."

Jill turned toward the voice. In a rectangular cage set back off the main field two boys in Wildcat jerseys were playing catch. The one who was standing up on a pile of dirt was throwing the ball to the one who was squatting.

"I'm sorry," she said stepping closer, "I didn't know."

The boy—well, he wasn't really a boy, he was a student after all, at least eighteen—raised his left leg up so high to his chest it kissed the drape of his blinding, white jersey. Jill could not say for sure what happened next, but he lunged like a spring trap and the ball blurred, and then she heard it, for the very first time. That guttural leather thud. Like falling into a library chair at Oxford, only harder, and infinitely more primal.

75

Her eyes danced back to the face of the boy—the man, really—who had spoken those words, thrown that ball, made that sound that was still reverberating in her neglected body.

"Are you the pitcher?" she heard herself ask.

There was a whoosh and a light slap, as if the ball this time had floated rather than raced.

"One of them," he said.

Maybe it was the lights, or the night air, or how long it had been since she'd done anything but dissect the thoughts and feelings of imaginary people, but the next thing Jill knew, she was stepping closer to the cage and forming the sentence, "I bet you're the best one."

The slab-thighed boy with the mask over his face put his hands between his legs and made some sort of fingering gesture to the pitcher. Tilting her head flirtatiously, Jill said, "I saw that."

The pitcher broke out in a lightly mocking grin. He threw the ball first—the ball always came first—then replied, "What? My signal for a curve?"

From behind her Jill heard a brusque shout, "McGaffey, you warm?"

His face went army-sober. "Yes, sir."

"Let's go." Noting Jill in proximity, the coach said, "Fans need to be in the bleachers. I don't want anyone back here distracting my players." Jill searched the pitcher's flint eyes as he ran past for signs that she'd succeeded, but found none.

It was a night for breaking rules. Staking out the ticket entrance, Jill threw in with a beer-sodden tribe of frat boys and slipped past the gate. Alone, as she was, it was not hard to find the perfect spot, one that framed the pitcher like a portrait between two poles. Never before had the simple act of staring at another human being brought her such pleasure. There was not an oafish jock bone in his perfect, lissome body. He was like something out of the ballet; grace and power coalescing in each stunning, liquid motion. Circling around to the back of the mound, he bent down over a dusty sack and cupped it in his palm, just so. Jill reminded herself to breathe as she traced the line of his calf, his thigh, the curve, the arch, the sprawl of his shoulders across which the letters read McGaffey, and straight up to the tiny sun-streaked curl against the back of his desert-browned neck.

There was a three-game series that weekend. Jill went to all of them, arriving earlier, staying later, thumbing casually through the program she bought each night so she could stare at his photo: Clem McGaffey, 6' 2" RHP, Freshman. She was sustained by a single blush. On the very first night, as he walked off the mound at the end of his outing, he dared to look up toward the stands. There was no scanning motion, no sense of searching; he knew exactly where she was. For three infinite seconds he held Jill's gaze. The fence turned to mist. Eighty feet became a dimple's width as all around her the sanguine fans bore secret witness to the glorious instant when the world of Jill Oberdorf thawed, and baseball became a word she could no longer say without smiling.

Even on the nights Clem McGaffey remained in the dugout, Jill was happy to be there. There was something in the green. Something languid and lush and undemanding. How lovely it was on a balmy spring evening to sit idly by as the batters swung and missed, swung and hit, swung and got hold of a piece that sent spirits soaring out under the wide lights, moonbound, transcendent, hearts lifted under the spell of the popped corn and the floodlit grass and the cheers of a thousand Wildcat fans. Jill leapt to her feet and actually screamed! For the first time in her orphaned, book-bent life, she was a part of something bigger than her own fertile cerebral cortex.

It was not until the final out of the final game of the series that they spoke. The giddy fans had dispersed to carry on their celebrations, the high-flying players emerging in twos and threes from the dugout. Clem was one of the last to appear. He came out alone, not looking up, not checking the stands, but heading straight for them, hurdling the cement steps two at a time before coming to rest in the empty seat beside her. With an amorous and complicit grin, he said, "Big baseball fan, huh?"

One lazy, exhilarating game spilled into the next. Jill followed the team on the road, blank pages left blank as she abandoned her brain for the tangible joy of her own forgotten body. Jill ran. Jill swam. Jill hurdled the Wildcat bleachers three at a time. Bliss was no longer cerebral, abstract, but the very real sensation of her own naked bottom growing sinewy beneath Clem's cupped palm. From March till the last day of August, she read nothing but the Sports Section by day and the sonnets of John Donne by night, recited from the crook of Clem's damp arm as he dozed, post-coitus. The sound of her voice he said soothed him.

They said good-bye without plans. The fall was a series of phone calls holding them together, weaning them apart—Jill couldn't say for sure which—capped off in November with an invitation to join Clem in Tucson for Thanksgiving. His mom and dad were coming out for the week, putting him up at their hotel. There would be a white terry cloth robe with her name on it.

Clem's parents were already seated in the Hacienda Dining Room when Clem and Jill made their tousled, belated entrance. Unsettled by the pinkish, smudged appearance of Jill's mouth, Gabby McGaffey sat up straight, and fast on the heels of hello said, "Clem tells us you have a wonderful job in Los Angeles."

Jill took a sip of her ice water in an attempt to cool her mischievous lips. "Well, I'm not sure I'd call it wonderful—"

Gabby interrupted to clarify. "But you do have a contract?"

"Mo-om."

Jill squeezed Clem's hand before withdrawing her own. Any urge to giggle had been thwacked clear out of her like wrinkles from an air-dried sheet. "If you're concerned about my being a distraction, Mrs. McGaffey, don't be. I would never do anything to jeopardize Clem's baseball career."

"See, mom, what did I tell you. Jill's my biggest fan."

Gabby opted to overlook the slight in light of the great relief. Lifting her salted glass to the center of the table, she smiled magnanimously. "To Clem's future."

Jill was quick to raise her glass and echo the sentiment. "To Clem's future."

The men followed suit, four arms upholding the dreams of one. "To Clem's future."

The waiter arrived with platters of food set down in the center of the table, family-style. There was a small turkey slathered in mole sauce, and stuffing with chipotle and Mexican sausage. There were corn meal patties with dollops of guacamole and sour cream, and cinnamon-crusted sweet potatoes, and fire-roasted red peppers in lime. There was nothing, not a crisp of skin, not a heap of mushed dressing that might transport Jill for an instant to her own Ohio childhood. "Excuse me," she said, and stifling a tear, ran to the hotel bathroom where a squat brown woman handing out mints and towels and sanitized combs held Jill in her arms till the trembling stopped.

That Christmas Jill was alone in her small, drape-dimmed apartment in L.A. when Clem's bright young face appeared on an NCAA Players-to-Watch special on TV. A reporter had interviewed him at his family home in Nashville. He sat on the sofa, bookended by his parents, and framed beneath the gilded star on the picture-perfect tree in the background. Gabby, petite and elegant in the broad awning of her son's shoulders, had smoothed the tip of his collared shirt and said in a way evocative of mystery that her son "had a gift."

Shortly thereafter, Jill vomited up the first portents of her future. For weeks she couldn't keep anything down. Spirit and resolve tottered within her spectral frame, until, on the final day of the winter break, on the eve of her return to the classroom and all its demands, she draped a shawl across her shoulders and, hunched over the desk that had been passed down through the Oberdorf family for three generations—all of them gone—worked on a hundred drafts of a letter. A thousand subtle variations on how this might turn out all right. *Maybe I could just...maybe later if you want you—*

In the end only silence, and the knowledge that she loved him, rang true.

Nine years later.

Rising up from the dry earth of the Sonoran Desert, the Picture Rocks were stacked like totem poles, their primitive tales of archaic longings forever etched in the terra cotta stone. Gabby considered the petroglyphs each morning en route to the summit. How daily questing men, whose remains had long been turned to dust, had prayed in pictures and chants for the blessing of fresh meat, an enemy slain, a change of heart in the mercurial rain gods. How, daily, they had recorded the history of man's infinite climb in the rocks that mounted skyward like a child's bouldered dream of Jacob's Ladder.

It was a mile to the top of the ridge. Breathlessly Gabby paused before the panorama: the scrubby, cactus-studded hills, the cool, alpine green high across the valley, the river bed, bone dry and dappled with unfathomable colorbursts of periwinkle and sun and flame, and to the east, the crested butte adorned with roughhewn crosses where the monks from the local monastery were laid to rest. In the distance she could hear the chime of the noon bell. Gabby waited for them to cross, two by two, from the low adobe bungalows of the cloister to the stone chapel at the center of the square.

In their long, brown robes, the monks began to appear. Gabby quickly scavenged the earth for a piece of charred shale and, withdrawing a pristine baseball from her pouch, began to scrawl her daily plea on the soft, white leather. *Pray for Clem McGaffey*. There were still monks in the courtyard, crossing. If only she could throw a little harder, a little farther. Like an outfielder with a play at home, she hurled it toward the blinding, cloud-wisped sky, watched it plummet pointlessly in the desolate ravine with the others.

After all this time someone should have noticed. One of them should have looked up, waved, shouted a word of encouragement that might echo through her day. Even Latin would have sufficed, but the silence felt personal. Bidding the monks a swift trip to an even hotter clime, Gabby brushed the charcoal from her fingers and turned to face with defiance her descent on the gravely trail.

Even at fifty-eight, she still had the body of a dancer. She wore her silvery blonde hair pulled back in a tight bun, just as she had as a junior ballerina with the Joffrey ballet. Once powdery and delicate, her face was now as brown as mitt leather, her sun-dried skin taut against fine, patrician bones. In a black maillot by a pool in Palm Beach, she would be taken for aristocracy, but here, in the Tucson outpost of Cortaro, Arizona she was thought of, if at all, as the pitcher's mom.

Gabby McGaffey was nothing if not a survivor. Through her teens, she had endured the daily suffering—the anorexic rations, the mutant, bunioned toes—that came with a dancer's pursuit of excellence. At twenty, she had yielded to the intransigent truth that no matter how many thousands of girls she was better than there were still those whose gifts were larger, and no amount of sacrifice or desire would ever make her their equals. Later, as the wife of a Classics professor at Vanderbilt, she survived the abstruse one-upmanship of the faculty cocktail circuit, the ubiquitous whine of country music, and a 42-hour, epidural-less labor. She had survived the PTA, Little League, Pony League, Wooden Bat League, high school play-offs, college scouts, and her husband's mid-life crisis.

His quest to stave off mortality had not manifested itself in the usual erotic forms but in the delusion that what he was really meant to do was write. An eighth-of-a-page ad in the back of *Poets & Writers* led to a request for a sabbatical and a sudden move to a Tara-like manse—"A Faulknerian Paradise" the ad had said—available asap. The furniture had not even arrived from Nashville when, throwing open the rose-glass-paned windows of the mahogany-shelved room he'd decided would change his life, he'd dropped dead of a heart attack. Gabby, staring out at the moon through the beards of Spanish moss, sat down on the empty floor and, ever the pragmatist, wept at the thought of all those unpacked boxes.

There must be a plan. Contrary to the evidence and her own temporal heart, Gabby had no choice but to believe that it was a good one. The alternative, that she had survived all this merely to wither and die on the sweat-slick seats of the Arizona Triple-A Sidewinders while ticking off her twenty-seven-year-old son's numbered days, was unthinkable.

Plans change.

Everyone said Clem was the most promising young talent the Dodger organization had seen in years. A pitcher who hit so well he even strengthened the lineup. They were certain he'd blaze through the farm system. Don't even bother settling in they said. Gabby had joked about coming to live with him when he got his big house in Beverly Hills.

Plans change. That's what the assistant manager of the Vero Beach Single-A Dodgers had said the day they traded Clem's contract—not even man for man, but in a dispensable heap—to the Cubs. He had two days to report to Lansing, Michigan. Gabby had flown down to help him drive his trailer north; to restock the fridge, do his laundry, figure out all the ways (it seems so obvious now!) that Chicago was where he was meant to play all along. She was drying the last of the new Cubs juice glasses when she felt her son's hot, salt breath against her back.

"You never watch me pitch anymore."

Gabby froze. She had watched him pitch. She had logged so many hours at so many games, her fanny had molded itself to the shape of a bleacher plank. She wouldn't trade an inning of it, but now, in the antebellum mansion where circumstances had flung her, she'd just begun to refashion a new life, and it was hers, and it was real. Covering the grand dining room with mirrors, she'd transformed it into a private studio for ballet. All the most precocious young dancers in the greater Monroe County area wanted to train with her, to rub up against her Joffrey mystique. Long, full days, resonant with concertos and the lithe movements of aspiring, lean-limbed girls awaited her back in Georgia. Yes, she wanted to see her son pitch. At night. On TV. While she sipped a mint julep in a hammock chair on the upper porch where, along the rose-paned doors, she grew herbs in a pot she bought along the Natchez Trace.

When in doubt, check the eyes. To look only at Clem McGaffey's sculpted physique it was impossible to imagine any distribution of weight or power other than his tiny mother being hoisted up in his deft hand and twirled in the air like a sequined doll. But to look into his eyes, the way they narrowed and flexed and quite nearly lunged at her knees, Gabby knew: his Sisyphean dream would die there and then if someone didn't help him carry it. At least for a while. Just a few weeks or so. What was a month or two compared to the happiness of her only child? Without breaking off from his beggarly gaze, Gabby began to formulate a list: call students, reroute mail, have neighbor take the new basil. In the grand scheme of things it was only a slight delay she decided, and lifting her hand to her son's damp cheek said, "I would love to stay and see you pitch."

Five years and as many teams later, they pulled into a

motor court in the desert flats of Cortaro, Arizona and, in the void where the rumble of motor and muffled truths had played out like background music across the country, Gabby declared it the end of the road.

Home, sweet, home.

Gabby was greeted upon return from her hike by flies swarming the breakfast dishes. Gripping the edge of the sink she unleashed a yeasty, mauled-by-coyotes howl. A lone strand of gray was loosed in the excitement. Summoning composure, she smoothed it back into place and proceeded in a martyr's trance to remove from the sink her grown son's yolky plate and his oatmealed bowl and his orange-pulped cup and his milk-skinned coffee mug, and began, once again, to clean up his mess.

Outside, the vroom of a truck announced Clem's return. Gabby closed her eyes, envisioning the tire-churned dirt drifting thoughtlessly toward the clothesline. There was no glory in this dust. It was not like the theatrical torrents that stormed at home plate after a slide, when all the fans held still for the call and the chance for half of them to show their disdain for it. This was dirt, plain and simple, loose and airborne and settling in filmy layers on every resident surface. Gabby wondered sometimes why she even bothered to wash her hair when an hour later it was as chalk-stiff as horsetails.

The door squawked and Clem stepped inside, filling the space they referred to with waning affection as the living room like a bass in a goldfish bowl. "Open that door back up," Gabby snapped, "I'm trying to get these flies out of here." Clem stepped down, undid the latch. "And you better not have gotten those clothes dirty, because I am not washing them again."

Clem placed his dexterous hand on Gabby's shoulder. The boyish spark that had once hinted at limitless horizons was no longer discernible; it had, over the years, been weight-trained and scrutinized and passed over and pressure cooked right out of him. "The clothes are fine, mom."

"I mean it, Clem. I am not your maid. When you leave this house, you leave it with a clean kitchen, you understand me?"

She should have been stricter on him growing up. She should have yelled at him more and cheered for him a little less. She should have left him alone in that mud lot in Lansing, come what may. She knew it. Knew she was not blameless in their predicament; in the fact that their mutual lives had been reduced to the numeric value of Clem's daily efforts and the sadistic promise that the great cosmic payoff was only a game away. Still, as if holding vigil at the bedside of the comatose, she waited each day for a miracle, or a sign that love required something new.

"I'm sorry," Clem said. "Coach called. He wanted me to come out to the field early."

Change plucked the air like a sitar string. Gabby turned off the faucet and, in the charged silence, asked, "Why?"

"Some press showed up. It was a last minute thing. I guess they wanted to talk to me."

Suddenly the clean, stacked Diamondback dishes gleamed. "Really?'

Clem slid into the bench seat of the breakfast nook and fanned open the Sports Section. "It was just local news. Channel 8."

"Still, they asked for you specially."

"Well, I am starting tonight..."

"They waited around until you got there," Gabby said, continuing to frame her view. "They don't do that for just anyone."

"They didn't exactly wait around. They interviewed a bunch of the guys."

"Like who?"

"I don't know. I wasn't there."

"Any other pitchers?"

"I don't know. None that I saw."

"Maybe they know something."

"Who?"

"The reporters." Positioning herself like a dubious proctor over Clem's shoulder, Gabby scanned the baseball page for clues.

Clem turned and smirked. "Yeah, or maybe they just have airtime to fill."

"Don't be negative. For all we know there's been a shakeup in Phoenix. That new kid they just traded in—what was his name?—he didn't look very good the other night.

Maybe he's going on the DL. Or maybe they've finally realized he just doesn't have the maturity for the job." Gabby zeroed in on Clem's shoulder. "How's the arm today?"

"Good."

"No soreness?"

"Nope."

Gabby had come to read the peaks and valleys of that small denial like a polygraph. There were uncertain no's and wishful no's and no's so full of terror she couldn't bare to ask again. After twenty years and five surgeries, she'd heard them all. Deeming this one reliable, she allowed hope to breathe once again. "You want to go over some tapes before tonight?"

"I'm good."

She shifted hips and asked again. "You sure?"

"You think I should?"

"Couldn't hurt. How 'bout you cue up the tape from the last Fresno game. I'll get your steak thawing."

"Okay."

"You think you're going to want one potato or two?"

"One's good."

"Broccoli?"

"Yeah, thanks." With a resonant tenderness, Clem called her back, "Mom?"

"Yes?" Gabby held her breath.

"Could you melt some cheese on it, please?"

"Sure," Gabby said, and turning toward the shelf where

the box of tapes of every game her son had played in the past five years was stored, she began to rifle through it, feverishly humming no particular tune.

Schadenfreude.

On the days he was scheduled to pitch, nothing trumped Clem's physical or emotional well being. The air conditioning in the trailer was turned off so as not to chill his arm; the radio, too, so as not to distract him with any unflattering pre-game predictions. Clem draped a bite of steak across a pool of A-1 and chomped down. He was humming the same noteless tune that had been in the air all day, the sonic current of quavering neurons.

Gabby wiped the sweat from her neck and chose her words like footsteps in a minefield. "So," she said, "I went over the scouting reports earlier. Fresno's leadoff batter's been in a bit of a slump. I think if you just hold them early on, get yourself a little cushion on offense, you'll be in good shape." It didn't matter that her strategy was tantamount to saying *why don't you just get the lead and keep it*, Gabby felt it was essential to offer something in the way of informed advice.

The grinding hum sparked and rasped. Gabby took a swig of her iced tea and changed the subject. "Did I tell you I got an e-mail from Lydia Hudson. Evidently, Davey failed the bar for the third time."

At this, Clem fell silent. "What's he going to do now?"

"I don't know. She didn't say."

Gabby had intended this update on failing peers to be

encouraging. It certainly had been for her. Not since the Christmas letter from the wife of the Dean of the College of Economics at Vanderbilt, informing friends that their twenty-nine year old son had moved back home to "regroup," had she gotten so much pleasure out of a correspondence.

"He was going to be my agent, remember that?" Clem said. "Seventh grade. We had it all figured out. I was going to make it to The Show and he was going to handle all my deals."

Clem shook his head, and in that brief, nostalgic flicker, the whole of her son's glorious life flashed before her— at twenty, at twelve, at ten, and two, and all the way back to the day he was born: the day Gabby had chosen for him the name Clemens in the hope he might someday write as well as Mark Twain.

"Maybe he just wasn't meant to be a lawyer," Gabby said.

Betrayal bled pink across Clem's cheeks. "Or maybe he'll take it again and pass."

Gabby reached across the table for her son's hand. Clem gripped his plate and rose to clear it. Stoically, he turned on the water, opened the cupboard beneath the sink where the dish soap was—

"Don't worry about those," Gabby said.

"You sure?"

"Sure. You don't want to be rushed."

Clem kissed his mother on the crown of her graying

head and reached for his bag. "You coming tonight?"

"Do I have a choice?"

Clem turned cooly toward the screen door. "Yeah, you do."

The door swung shut. To the empty trailer, Gabby said, "I was just kidding." Sliding her sweat-slick thighs out from the vinyl, she raced to the screen. "Clem."

"Yeah."

"I have a good feeling about tonight." Beyond a womb and the need to be reassuring Gabby had no preternatural qualifications; still, she was convinced she had impacted the outcome of many a game with her willed prescience.

"You always have a good feeling, mom," Clem said and waved her off with a nod.

The care and feeding of an
11-year old ballplayer.

For Jill it was a matter of principle: the removing of crusts was something done for young children. Before they have teeth. Gus was league-age twelve. Life had crust and the sooner he got used to it the better. "Gus!" she called, removing the crispy, sugar-spiced slices of intact bread from the toaster oven. "Cinnamon toast is ready!"

The barstool met Gus at the hip. He no longer hopped up, but merely slid casually onto it. "Thanks."

"Do you have a lot of homework tonight?"

"I don't know. I don't think so."

"You don't think so? Where's your planner?" The very word still gave Jill shivers of organizational delight: all those double-starred assignments, the check marks of progress, those thick, time-lapse arrows that helped orchestrate the days before major exams.

"It might be at school."

"Not going to help you much there, now is it?" Jill sighed. "Alright, let's take it subject by subject. Math?"

"I did it in class"

"Spanish?"

"We just watched a video."

"Social Studies?"

There was a hiccup of pause and then, "It's nothing. I just have this one little part of this worksheet, that's all."

"How little?"

"Like two questions."

Jill wasn't sure if it was only her son or, in fact, all children who assessed the difficulty of a task by the amount of words in the question. How many times had these trivial remainders of worksheets turned out to be a request for the student to describe, in detail, the meaning of life. Please, be specific.

"Where's your backpack?" Sometimes she felt as if there were a giant medicine ball between them; try as she might to get Gus to hold it, he kept passing it back with a petulant groan. "I am telling you right now, you will never get through high school with this haphazard approach to your schoolwork. You need a system, do you hear me?" Her voice disappeared around the corner as she followed the trail of crumpled boxers, soiled socks, bunched tees, piling them up in her arms en route to the bed where Gus's backpack and all its secrets lay. From the depths of the blue nylon cavern, where fruit chew remnants and months-old reminder slips and assignment sheets worth 50% of the semester grade co-mingled in the dank and musky funk, Jill unearthed a startlingly familiar form. Lifting the spine up to the light, she gasped.

How long had she waited for this day to come? For the day when a book would be placed in her son's hand that would speak to the deepest longings of his striving heart. Had she been the one to suggest it, of course, it would have been rejected outright. This was better. This was perfect. An in-class reading of the book that epitomized grit, perseverance, doubt, loneliness, determination: old man vs. fish. Boy vs. batter. Surely he would see the connection.

If only she had more time. Why was it that these life-altering moments always seemed to arrive unannounced in the midst of the after-school rush? Tossing the weathered book on the counter with a papery thud, Jill said, cool as jazz, "What's this?"

Gus shoved a bale of sweet toast in his mouth and offered a garbled, "Itsabook."

Jill tilted her head to one side with such feverish nonchalance she almost pinched a nerve. "Have you started it already?"

"We finished it today in class."

"Oh." Jill counted back the days he had failed to mention they were reading it at all. Perhaps the metaphors had left him speechless. "So, how did you like it?"

"Um," he said wiping the crumbs from his mouth with his blue baseball shirtsleeve. "It's okay. Can you get the knots out of my cleats please?"

Jill was grateful to have a place to hide her eyes. "Well, I mean, I don't need a full analysis or anything, honey, I just thought you could tell me a little bit about it."

"Haven't you ever read it?"

"Yes, I've read it."

"So..."

"Well each reader brings something different to the material. That's what's so magical about books. That's why literature is really the most essential component of a—" Jill caught herself transitioning into lecture mode, shifted her energy back to the knots. "I just wondered what you thought, that's all."

"It's about an old man who goes fishing," he said and chugged his milk half-clean. "That's about it."

Nimbly she loosened the laced knots. "Anything else?"

"Well there was one good part where this kid who knows the old man, and some other guys, they listen to the baseball games on the radio. They're in Cuba, I think. Lot of good ball players in Cuba. Plus he talks about DiMaggio a lot, so that's cool."

It was all her fault. In her desperation to convert an apathetic reader, Jill had found her last, best hope in the adult biographies of old-time ballplayers. She had allowed her son to spend his formative preadolescent years with Babe Ruth and Rube Waddel and Moses Fleetwood Walker, with men who spit and swore and downed sour mash and blood-rare, fist-thick steaks for breakfast. While his classmates were skipping merrily through *Captain Underpants*, Gus was reveling in the tales of hooch hounds and bar brawlers, gamblers and game throwers, golden-armed gods who pitched straight games for the win only to die broken and penniless and more often than not, in the arms of syphilitic hookers. Still, it was ink on vellum. She had gotten her son to touch the pages alone in the flashlit dark, to scan the printed word with his very own ravenous eyes, to feel his insides stir and leap at an image, a memory, a moment-transmitted from the writer's to the reader's mind like the best secret ever.

"Well, forget about the story for a minute," Jill said, so casually her blasé brow nearly froze near the hairline. "What do you think about the old man?"

Gus shrugged.

"C'mon, Gussy, three things about him."

His shoulders strained under the considerable weight of his English-teacher-mother heritage and sighed. "He's really sunburnt, and really wrinkled, and he's like, totally obsessed with that fish."

"Well, honey," Jill said, handing over cleat number one. "It's more than just a fish."

"I know, I know. It's like the biggest fish in the universe."

"No. I mean, the story's about more than just a fish."

"Not really, mom." Gus tugged his laces tight and double-knotted them. "That's all he talked about the whole time."

"Okay, all right." Cleat number two was caked in dried

dirt. Jill whacked it against the edge of the kitchen sink to free it. "So that's all he talks about, and all he thinks about. And all he cares about is catching that giant fish. Does that remind you of anything?" Taking a jelly knife from a juice cup left in the sink since breakfast, Jill prodded the dirt from the rubber spike. "Maybe something from your own life?"

"If you're talking about me and baseball, mom, forget it." Gus tilted his head back, dropped the soggy bread in his open gullet and chewed before adding, "Fishing is not a sport."

"I think Hemingway would disagree."

"Who?"

"Ernest Hemingway," Jill said, pulling the second lace so hard she split a nail. "The author of the book we're talking about."

"Oh, yeah, right. But it still doesn't have anything to do with me. First of all, I'm not old. Second of all, I'm not on a losing streak—I mean this guy hadn't caught a fish in like a year or something. I'm averaging nine strikeouts a game." Snidely, Gus tossed in an aside. "And it would be a lot more if you'd let me throw a curve ball."

Jill handed over the second shoe. "No curves till you're fourteen. Period."

Gus glared. "Plus, I'm a Starter. Starters just have to—" He lifted his fingers in the form of ironic quotes, —'catch the fish'. They don't have to 'bring him in.' That's what Closers are for." Jill felt the side of her lip twitch as if dancing upward.

"See, just because I think it's a dumb story doesn't mean I can't make up some blah-blah-blah for the book report."

"Gus Oberdorf" she said trying to override the urge to laugh. *The Old Man and the Sea* is one of the greatest stories every written. Are you telling me there isn't anything you liked about it?"

Flashing a firecracker smile, Gus said, "It's short."

Just the facts ma'am.

For many people, the two-inch column of newsprint known as the box scores could cue up an entire game, play by play, blue sky and all, but not Jill; for her the encryptions were impenetrable. Players did not leap from the page. Home runs, typeset in black, did not fly over the wall of her mind. One time, she did get the distinct impression that the numbers were sticking their tobaccoey tongues out at her, but beyond that, they were, for her, about as lively and accessible as an annual report.

"Well, today's the day," Jill announced waving her spanking new score book optimistically as she climbed up the major Dodger bleachers. "Today it's all going to click!"

Beatrix did not look up from the official stat book as Jill took a seat beside her. The years at North Palms had been good to Beatrix, if not to her son, Ian, whose promotion into the major division was due entirely to age. Gone was the clueless Brit who once referred to the outfield as "that large grassy area," and, in her stead, a sort of statistical punk-goddess of the stands. Opposing teams consulted her regularly. Games under protest often hinged on her say. Beatrix flipped the Tootsie Pop from one side of her mouth to the other and with her silver-studded tongue said, "You don't have do this you know, luv."

The year before, Gus had been edged out of a spot on the 11/12 year old all-stars because some other kid's dad came in waving a stat book that proved somehow that his kid's batting average was better than three or four other kids' on the team. Gus didn't happen to be one of them but that didn't seem to matter; someone had to go. Gus would get his chance the next year. Gus hadn't been there as long as the other kids. Gus's family didn't really contribute much to the league. And so it was, on a perfect June day, that her son stood with all his buddies at the end-of-the-year picnic, his t-shirt sopped from water balloons and squirt guns and sodas shaken with glee, hair dripping in spikes off his guileless lashes as fourteen other names were called. Names of kids he struck out lots of times. Names of kids whose dads were coaches or assistant coaches or who at least knew how to pose in nylon wind shirts at games. "Yes I do," Jill replied. "I need to learn this."

"Well I'm just entering the lineup now. So give me a minute."

Jill watched as Beatrix wrote the name Oberdorf on the fifth line. "I think you made a mistake. Gus always goes before Ronchack."

Beatrix lifted her eyes from beneath the shade of her official Dodgers stat girl cap and said, through a curtain of hennaed pigtails, "Coach moved him down."

"Why?"

"He can't keep batting cleanup when he's struck out—"

Beatrix flipped officiously through the pages of the book and made a quick tally. "—twelve times in the last eight games."

Jill had noticed Gus wasn't hitting as often as he usually did but, to reduce it to that: just numbers. No stories, no explanations. No word picture of how his coltish body had uncoiled itself like a discus thrower as he swung for the fences. If they wanted a real record of a game they should record the narrative in prose.

"Alright," Jill said. She stared down the tiny, foreboding squares of the stat book like a Bible transcriber at the head of a pin. "So, if the batter gets on, I mark it here, right?"

"Only if he gets a single. If it's a walk you write BB." Sensing the pause in Jill's pen, Beatrix clarified. "Base on Balls."

"And all the positions have little numbers, right? 1 is, of course, first base."

Out came the lollipop with an admonishing wave. "No. First base is 3. Remember?"

"Oh, that's right. Okay, so first is 3 and second is 2—"

"Second is 4. The catcher is 2."

Suddenly it was all clear: there was a secret baseball decoder ring and everyone had one but her. Jill erased a mark on the tiny blue square and corrected herself. "Okay, so first is 3, and second is 4, and the catcher is 2, and the pitcher is number 1—that's right." That one, at least, made sense.

Beatrix rattled off the list impatiently. "And third is 5 and shortstop is 6 and the outfield is 7,8,9, left to right. Easy-peazy-lemon-squeezy." The umpire crooked his finger through the fence and Beatrix leapt to her feet. "Excuse me," she said, smoothing the flares of her short, pleated, schoolgirl-gone-bad skirt. "Blue needs me."

How did she do it? How had she come to say the word Blue aloud with confidence when Jill still struggled with the impulse to call him the referee? How was it that it was Beatrix who was feeding the folded lineup sheet through the fence to the new (and not entirely unattractive) ump like a phone number and flipping that damn lolly around in her mouth like she was the Queen of North Palms, when everyone knew they didn't even sell lollipops at the North Palms snack bar!

Jill furrowed. Perhaps if Beatrix paid a little more attention to her own son, who spent most of the game blowing snot bubbles out of his nose and gumming up the other kids' bats, the Dodgers wouldn't be in second place. Maybe if she played catch with him at home or got him some private lessons, or (Jill had heard some of the parents suggest) kept him home for a game or two, they would be spared his tragic attempts at hand-eye coordination and could beat those damn Yankees and move into first!

Blue and Beatrix and the Dodgers took their respective places and the opposing Cardinals first batter stepped into the box. Jill smoothed her pristine page of tiny blue squares. She jutted her neck out. She held her pencil like an accelerator foot at the starting line and leaned forward. A pencil tapped on her score pad. "Numbers won't mean anything without the names, luv," Beatrix said. "This is Graef. Number 7."

Jill looked down for the amount of time it took to write a name and number and missed the first pitch. The ump let out an indecipherable grunt that had the specific phonetic make-up of neither the word "ball" nor "strike." If she had to guess, Jill would have said it was "Haip!" Craning discreetly, she saw Beatrix make a tiny slash mark in a short row of two boxes that sat on a slightly longer row of three, in the upper corner of the individual scoring square. "Was that a strike?"

"Straight over the plate," Beatrix said cooly.

Jill knew what a strike was, for God's sake. Her son threw them all the time.

The second pitch was tossed and Blue made his call. "Haip!" Jill placed a confident slash in the second strike box.

Beatrix scowled. "That was a ball."

"That was ball? It sounded just like the strike." Most of the umps indicated strikes by pointing their fingers or chopping their hands or jerking their elbows back like slot machine levers. Some of them even said the word "strike" out loud and clear as day. This guy seemed to be practicing some sort of umpire/tai chi.

"Similar," Beatrix responded, the white stick waggling in her one-uppity mouth.

The third pitch crossed the plate. The batter hit the ball straight to Gus who, having pitched all six innings the game before, was now, to Jill's great relief, playing shortstop; she could eat when Gus played short. Gus picked up the ball and threw it to the first baseman who caught it for the first out of the game. On the official pad the play was described in its entirety with a 6-3 in the center of the blue-lined diamond and a 1 in the out column. Jill, too, made a 1 in that column, but opted instead to write in the center diamond, Gus 0. makes the out! It just seemed so much clearer.

Beatrix leaned over and burst out laughing. "Oh Jill, for heavens sake, it's not a diary. Why don't you just leave the scorekeeping to me and go enjoy the game?"

The specter of Ian in an all-star jacket suddenly loomed. Even meritocracies were susceptible to corruption at the hands of an ex-patriot divorcee in tight pants. Who knew what sort of numbers might finagle their way onto Ian's year-end stat sheet? Who knew which coaches might feel indebted to review it? Jill tucked her score book under her arm and proceeded down the bleachers. "Thanks for your help, Bea. I think I can take it from here."

Jill was halfway down before she lost her battle with lesser urges. "Just let me know when Ian is up. I still get a little confused when the subs come off the bench."

The words hung like a green fog as Jill stepped blindly over the edge of the next plank and toppled—fanny, thigh,

108

elbow—finally coming to rest akimbo on the second row. A small, quiet man on the bottom bleacher was the only one to offer a hand. His last name, Jill knew, was Urbino. His son Mario was the Dodger's other starting pitcher. Jill had often wondered if he wasn't just a little bit better than Gus. Through stung cheeks, she said, "Thank you."

By the time she'd blotted her scraped forearm with a damp paper towel from the bathroom, there was a runner on second and another one moving towards first base. He wasn't moving very fast, so it must have been a walk. A good ol' WK. Or maybe he was hit. Or maybe he was just a really slow runner. Leaning over toward Mr. Urbino, she whispered, "Was that a walk?"

"Hit," he said.

Jill grimaced. "He hit the ball, or the ball hit him?"

Mr. Urbino swatted his own arm to demonstrate. In gnat-sized letters Jill wrote, Mario hit the batter and shook out her hand. Halfway through the first inning and already she was exhausted. She didn't want to watch like this. She wanted to gaze out dreamily at the field and clap and cheer and when things started to happen all at once and quickly, she wanted to hold her breath and wait for someone to tell her how it'd all turned out.

The Dodger catcher stepped out over the plate. Lifting his mask like knight's armor, he shouted, "Two down!" Gus followed suit, holding up two fingers to the outfield. Two outs.

Good news. Except to Jill, who only had one recorded in her book. Frantically tracing the page like vertical Braille, she missed the first pitch to the new batter, missed the Cardinal hitting the ball, missed the ball traveling hard and long through Gus's path and straight out to center field. The robust cheers on the other side called her back to the field where the red-sleeved arms of the opposing coaches were flailing like air traffic controllers under duress.

The Cardinal kids ran in, one, then another— she couldn't tell you their names. Gus held up his hands to cutoff the throw from the center fielder, but it was too late. There were no more runners to catch. Jill waited for the murmurings on the bench to form themselves into an explanation, something with a beginning and a middle and an end. A fellow Dodger mom, one who'd taken up scorekeeping during the Great American Smoke-out and never stopped (scorekeeping that is, smoking she went back to the next day), turned back from her nylon sling chair on the ground and shouted, "You markin' that as an error?"

"E6," Beatrix shouted back.

Did she say 6? Wasn't 6 the shortstop? Wasn't that Gus? Jill was just about to ask Mr. Urbino when the scorekeeper from the other team arrived. Tipping her visor in Beatrix' direction she confirmed, "Error on the shortstop, right?"

"It seemed perfectly playable to me," Beatrix said.

What was this? Subjectivity in the game of cold, hard

facts. Looking up at the opposing mother, Jill attempted to stem the tide. "Looked like a bad hop to me."

"You see a hop, Bea?"

"No hop. It's a simple E6F—fumble by the shortstop."

"Oberdorf, right?"

"Yes, Number 21. Gus Oberdorf."

Jill wanted to shout out every good, right thing her son had ever done, not only on the field, but at home: the ceramic pen holder he'd made with *I love You, mom* inscribed on the bottom, the citizenship awards he'd won three times this year, the way he always put his hand on her shoulder as he sat down for dinner and asked about her day. Jill shut the scorebook. She couldn't do it. Wouldn't do it. All-stars be damned, she would not be a party to recording for posterity the mistakes of preadolescent children. Looking up at the opposing score mom, she said icily, "It's the first error he's made all year."

Over the top of Jill's head, Beatrix and the Cardinal score mom exchanged arch glances and began flipping back through their specious books to confirm.

111

Twelve.

When I grow up I'm going to be a writer. I'm going to live in a little house with a big tree outside my window that has leaves that change color in the autumn and fall off in the winter and then, in the springtime, turn green and have blossoms and berries and birds' nests. I'm going to wear my pajamas every day and drink hot chocolate from a thermos that I'll keep by my desk so I don't have to leave the room to go to the kitchen. I'll write every single day except for on Sundays. On Sundays, I'll go out to the movies and just sit there all day eating popcorn in the dark and dreaming about different lives. One thing I know for sure is I want to write my books the old-fashioned way, with a feather pen and a pot of ink and a blotter. I know it takes longer but the people who wrote that way seemed to write better things. I'm not sure yet exactly what I'm going to write about. Definitely not about horses or outer space or sports. Yuk! I guess what I really want to write about is why people are who they are and if they're just born that way or if life makes them that way somehow. Like Anne Frank. She said you can't believe in things being meant to be unless you believe in God and I think she's right about that. Sometimes I think I may have some good, big purpose in me, too, but I don't want to believe what she believed cause I don't want to die young. I don't want to just write one book even if it is a really good one that everyone in the whole world reads and loves and talks about. I think I'd rather be alive and write lots of books even if they aren't quite as popular. But I don't know. I'm only twelve. Maybe when I'm really old—like thirty—I'll think that writing one great book is plenty.

All roads lead to June.

By the end of May, the biweekly games were no longer just recreational matches enjoyed by the families of the players on the two opposing teams. They were fights to the play-off death, providing for its spectators a level of fervency rivaling the gladiatorial bouts of Rome. Jill had been embarrassed at first, going up to the field to watch games her son wasn't even in. She was just dropping off her check for Casino Night she would say if anyone asked. But no one ever did as, inning by inning, families would arrive from work, from school, from a sibling's clarinet lesson, converging en masse atop the good, green hill that rose up from the tight, urban grid and called them together under the warm, dry, guava-tinted sky. Chili cheese fries for all!

Everyone had their reasons for being there: to see a threat eliminated, a starting pitcher exhaust his innings, a best friend succeed, an enemy fail; to avoid making dinner, or starting homework, or the dream-squeezing vice of four tight walls. Along the outfield fence the men gathered. The dreams they arrived with had not come to pass. In grunts and scoffs they commiserated, certain that it would have all turned out differently—life, Little League—if only they had been calling the plays.

Jill sat at a picnic table off to the side, a de facto neutral zone. She hadn't seen Gus since the second inning, when he and Zach Dempster had run off in search of Troy Jones's home run ball and never came back.

"Can I have some money?"

And so he returns. "May I?' Jill corrected. "Where have you guys been? You're missing a great game."

"Nah," Zach said with a swat. "These guys are fags. The only decent guy they've got is Troy. Him-an-me-an-you," he said, whacking Gus across the gut, "—an-Urbino-an-Larson, we're gonna kick ass in all-stars."

"Zach, you know I don't like that kind of—"

"Hey, where the hell you mutton chops been?" Rod Dempster came up behind the two boys and squeezed their necks as if trying to juice them. "I been waitin' for you in the bullpen. Goading Jill with a click of the cheek he said, "Gonna start gettin' their curve balls ready for all-stars."

"Gus is not throwing any curveballs, Rod." After four seasons in the same league, Rod Dempster was like family, like the toothpick-sucking stepbrother who shows up Christmas Eve fresh out of the joint. "So just drop it all right."

"C'mon, let me make a real pitcher out of this kid, wouldja?"

"If memory serves, he struck out thirteen of your players just last week." She didn't have to write it down in any book. She saw it happen, would never forget it. "I think he'll be okay."

"Still wasn't enough to beat ol' Rod though was it?" The fact that the Yankees had beaten the Dodgers 1-0, with an error on a double in the sixth, to clinch the season and the right to have Rod coach the all-star team, was still a matter of some contention: if there was justice in the world, the Dodgers would have won.

"C'mon, mom, please. I'm not a little kid or anything. I'm twelve years old."

"You're eleven years old, actually, and the answer is no. Not till you're fourteen." All the experts in all the books said thirteen, but Jill preferred to err on the side of safety. "You start throwing curve balls now, you won't have an arm left to pitch with by the time you get to high school. Is that what you want? Is it?"

"But mom, we could have like the best all-star team ever. We could go all the way to Williamsport, but I need to throw junk."

Jill hated that term. She didn't even know how it applied here, still, she was predisposed to reject it. "If you need any help with your pitching, we'll talk to your own coach about it."

"That guy's a fag," Zach said.

Rod swatted him on the biceps. Zach whelped, "What? That's what you said!"

"C'mon mom, he doesn't know anything. He's just a dad. Rod was a real pitcher. In the Majors. He made it all the way to AAA. Triple-A, mom. Do you know how good you have to be to play Triple-A ball?"

In the levee where restraint is calibrated, monitored, where floods of irrevocable words are held at bay, the cables collapsed, snaking out like lariats, kicking the wall of Jill's skull with flashes of blue flame. "For your information...." Safe in the chamber of her own mind she had braved the retort a thousand times, usually flinging it at Rod or Beatrix or some ump who couldn't recognize a pitched strike when he saw one, and always ending with Gus throwing his arms around her in a meringuey swirl of gratitude. Now, Jill froze. Lifting her fingers to her lips she came to understand that her mouth was open, that words had already escaped, and that her son was expecting more of them.

"For my information, what?" Gus asked.

Jill turned away as if she had lost something. Looking everywhere but her son's eyes, she mumbled. "For your information, uh, I won't be changing my mind about this, so, um, I would recommend you save your breath."

Gus kicked the dirt and stormed off. In his wake, Jill cupped her mouth and held it shut for dear life. Lately, the truth had been barking within her like acid reflux, churning on the back of her tongue, boxing her epiglottis as if for the right to pass. It was only a matter of time before it would overtake them both. Jill knew it. Her only hope was that when it did it was not on a day Gus was scheduled to pitch.

The play-offs.

Tournament brackets were nothing like box scores. There were no picky-oony details to fill in, no numbers, no subs, just a clean, progression of winners and losers that narrowed inexorably, and in a familiar three-act narrative form, to a single victor. The Dodgers would play the 3rd place Pirates on Day Two of the double-elimination tournament; the 1st place Yankees (why hadn't she comprehended the enormity of that one losing run?) would face the 4th place Cardinals in the opening game on Thursday. Win and the path would be short and sweet. Lose and play like a junkyard dog scrapping his way under the fence to freedom. Jill blocked off the calendar for every eventuality. Four teams. Six days in June. Oh, for the stories those lines would tell!

Thursday.

Jill had it all figured out. The end-of-the-year awards ceremony at Gus's school started at 5:00 pm. The Yankee/Cardinal game started at 5:30. All they had to do was swing by the school, pick up Gus's awards—three in all— and head straight for the field in time for the final innings. At 5:57, the President's Physical Fitness Awards were handed out. Gus was one of only three boys in his class to receive one, a high honor made even more glowing by the expediency with which it was distributed. The ribbons for the Geography Bee, in which Gus had taken a surprising third place, were handed out at 6:23. Two down, one to go.

That was an hour and seven minutes ago. Since then Jill had clapped politely for the Robotics Club Reps, the Glockenspiel Chorus, the AV corps, the Weeding & Composting Crew and the girl who volunteered 200 hours to help read to the blind. A retiring teacher Gus had never had was presented with an honorary gift basket of lotions and soaps for her four-and-a-half decades of service as a shaper of eight-year old minds. Letters were read, speeches were given, a phone call from the assistant-superintendent of the L.A. Unified School District was, after several failed attempts, patched in over the loud speaker. Jill checked her watch.

"I wonder who's winning?" she whispered to Gus who

was wriggling in the seat beside her.

"Gotta be the Yankees."

"Unless Zach had an off day."

"Or Cinfuego jacked one, bases loaded."

A pointy chin inserted itself between them. "SSHHHH!"

"And now for our Merit Roll winners..."

Jill held the camera in her lap as Gus hurdled the stairs to the lectern where the principal of the school, who had early on slotted him for failure, handed him a certificate for a 3.4 GPA. The tenth of a point that had kept him from the Honor Roll pressed against her like a barb. If only she'd been firmer about his nightly reading quota, his root and prefix cards, the mastermind math drills. If only she hadn't believed his teacher when she said the children were intended to do their Science Fair projects on their own.

"Pssssst!" Gus's bright, impish face appeared at the end of the aisle zapping the angst right out of her. "Let's go!"

Jill slid her metal chair back with such a fervent squawk it nearly toppled onto the irked parents behind her. "Sorry, excuse me," she said and giddily fled, son in hand, from the packed and fetid auditorium and out into the cool night air. The sky was blue-purple and deepening, the last hint of rusted light dipping its toes in the horizon. Even if extra innings had been required—their last best hope of catching any action—it was unlikely there would be light to play them. Gus slapped the dashboard like reigns on a sleigh, the need to know spreading through his limbs like a bad rash.

"There's no way they're still playing," Jill announced calmly as she gunned it through a yellow light. Speeding down the boulevard she rounded the bend that led to the road that cut through to the driveway where their poxing curiosity would at last be quelled. There was not a van in the lot. Gone too was the light. She pulled the car in till it nearly nudged the snack bar wall, bathing it in her high beams.

The announcement case was mounted on the other side. As if in the act of some collegiate prank, Jill and Gus tiptoed around the abandoned site, whispering in half-giggles. "I can't believe we're doing this," Jill said.

"Here, give me your flashlight."

Gus pointed the key chain light toward the board and together they traced the narrow, yellow beam like tomb raiders. Parsing the hieroglyphic markings of the Major Boys' Playoff Bracket, they fell silent. On the line that jutted out from the match-up between the indomitable Yankees and the fourth place Cardinals, it was the little birdies that found themselves on top.

Who to start, (or is it whom)?

Year after play-off year, Jill had sat among the baseball sophists as they pondered the question of the ages: Did the wise coach play his best pitcher in the first game and assure the team's place in the winner's bracket, or did he try to secure a win with his number two thrower and save the best for the more challenging games to come? Start with your number one boy and he'd be able to pitch again in game 7; a plus to be sure, unless your team never makes it past game 5. Baseball wisdom, disseminated by all the men who'd been burned by the temptation of the long view, was this: there was no game but today's.

To Jill the *when* was secondary. It was all about the who, the which, the one who ranked in the eyes of the Dodger manager and his two coaches as the go-to guy. It was conceivable that certain people might think of Mario as the better pitcher. That Mario was the more obvious choice to secure their spot in the winner's bracket. No doubt there were stats that could be enlisted for a side-by-side comparison if one were so inclined. And if one had the stats to do it. Jill took a sip of her Kahlua & milk and made peace with rejection. Saturday would be the better game to pitch anyway. Stepping straight onto the mound after a long, hard week of school was really too much to ask of a child. The second start, the sleep-in-and-have-a-good-breakfast-and-take-your-time-on-Saturday morning start, was really the way to go. Jill slurped on a milky ice cube till it lodged with a gasp in the back of her throat. Unless they lost game 1 and dropped down to the loser's bracket. Then it was do-or-die for the Saturday pitcher. Win or the season was over, a thought that propelled Jill straight up off the couch and into the doorway of Gus's room.

He was standing shirtless in the mirror, his front leg lunging forward, his pitching arm folded stealthily behind his back. The lines of his body, a virtual blueprint of Clem's, haunted her. When, without visible provocation, Gus turned suddenly and hurled a ball blindly in her direction, Jill could not help but think he'd read her mind.

Gus smiled to see her flinch. "It's just foam, mom."

Jill returned the ball and said, "It's getting kind of late."

"I've got twenty more minutes." Resuming his position, he scanned the perimeter like a gecko in fly's range.

"I meant for coach to call and you know, let you know his plans for tomorrow."

"I already know his plans."

"You do?"

"Yeah." Snapping left, he threw the ball back to the imaginary first base in his doorway.

"He called when you were in the shower."

"Well, what did he say?"

Gus returned Jill to his periphery. "I'm starting

123

tomorrow night."

Hot air balloons of joy rose up from the spot where once festering doubt had reigned. "Really? Gussy, that's great. Don't you think that's great?"

Gus tipped the visor of his Dodger cap to conceal his eyes. "You seem surprised."

"Well, no, it's not that I'm surprised," she blathered. "I mean, look at the year you've had. No— it's just exciting, that's all. Coach obviously thinks you're the team's go-to guy." Jill paused, scanned the roof of her mind. "Which means you're going to need a good night's sleep."

"One more," Gus said to the mirror, staring down the boy he was attempting to outgrow.

"What are you doing, exactly?"

With ventriloquist lips, Gus replied, as if even the minor movement of his mouth might somehow detract. "Practicing my pick-offs."

Jill lifted her hands to block her face as the final spin-and-toss was launched undetected. "I thought you're not allowed to do that till next year."

Gus smiled the length of a long road and said, "We're not."

The post-game show.

Not since the afterglow of labor and delivery had Jill experienced such a euphoric melding of pride and relief. A pocket of worry-free time seemed to be carved out of the surrounding air, as the next game's anxious pangs were held at bay in the outer ether. Withdrawing a bag each of peas and berries and succotash from the freezer, she closed the door and stood reveling in the newest entry on the bracket. Dodgers-7 Pirates-1. No longer speculation or hope or dream, but fact; the official recorded history of the North Palms Major Boys Play-offs, Chapter 1. The thrill, far from lessening with familiarity, managed to sink deeper into her skin with each take. Gus had thrown a two-hitter to help secure the Dodgers spot in the winner's bracket. The tournament was now theirs to lose.

Returning to the sofa, she spread the frozen food bags up and down Gus's arms like mud packs, one on the shoulder, one on the elbow, one on the wrist. "I don't need one here," Gus said, freeing the hand he used to operate the remote.

Jill held the bags in place with an oven mitt as they stared at the nightly sports report. Ordinarily it proved no more distracting than a sitcom in a foreign language—she could devise an entire lesson plan in her mind while never taking her eyes off the screen—but when the broad-chested man in the Italian suit described a pitcher's two-hitter as valiant, the commentary suddenly bloomed in her ears like poetry, rousing a hunger for more of whatever it was he knew. "Could you turn it up a little, please?"

Gus pumped his thumb on the volume button and, with a grin that seemed to have traveled through time and flesh, quipped. "Big baseball fan, huh?"

And then there were three.

Arriving to warm-up for the afternoon game on Saturday, Jill looked on as the Pirates went out for the season. One by one, the players peeled off their jerseys and piled them high in the arms of the team mom who reciprocated with Gatorade and a little sack of chocolate coins wrapped in gold: pirate booty. Before the last batting helmet was removed from the dugout, the Pirate kids had thrown in with a ragtag of friends in the weedy side lots for a rollicking game of Over the Line, while by the cars the Pirate parents, who had spent the last four months going hoarse to avoid this very fate, traced the arc of the tragedy: bad calls and a lopsided draft and coaches who never really had what it took.

Operation Gus.

On Sunday morning, Rod's Yankees beat the Cardinals, who had been forced into the loser's bracket by the Dodgers the day before, to earn a berth in the championship. Jill and Gus were there to see it, to bolster themselves with the knowledge that they, the Dodgers were the team to beat. "Well," she said, unsettled by the two Yankee home runs and their errorless play, "We're in the catbird seat now." The Yankees would have to beat the Dodgers twice to take the championship. The Dodgers would only have to beat them once. One win out of two. One win with a cushion. More margin of error than the mother of the player who'd have to pitch in a hypothetical game 7 could hope for.

The elimination of the Dodger advantage took less than two hours. Gus hadn't spoken since he struck out in the bottom of the sixth with the winning run on second. To an offer of chili cheese fries he'd simply shaken his head and slipped into the car where they now sat idling in the parking lot behind a clog of loitering, backslapping Yankees. Gus lowered his cap as the players peered through the windshield. Jill rolled down her window and teased, "Enjoy it while you can boys."

Gus didn't even utter an embarrassed protest.

"You want the radio?"

Gus shrugged.

"In n' Out?'

Nothing.

"You played a great game, Gussy. You know you did. You made a bunch of great plays at short. You had two doubles and a single—"

"It wasn't a single."

"Honey, I saw it. You hit the ball and got to first. That's a single, right?"

"Fielder's choice."

"Well, I don't know anything about that," Jill said, "But I think you're being too hard on yourself. One strike-out, that's all it was."

Gus cranked his head so far around toward the window she could study the mushroomy scruff of dirt along the back of his neck. Jill continued to theorize and spin: the team made too many errors, Mario didn't pitch his best, they'd just have to go back tomorrow and beat the pants off 'em. Waiting for the light to change, she stared at the fogged circle of hot breath in the glass beside his cheek; maybe if she held very still he would forget she was there, lift a finger to the window, trace a clue.

At home, Jill served him tomato soup on a tray in the bath. She let him play Nintendo on a weeknight. She made fresh chocolate chip cookies from scratch from the tub of dough she'd bought to raise money for the school computer fund. Gus ate one, Jill five. "Oh, good," she chimed as the techno-thumping montage of their favorite nightly sports show burst on the screen. Jill curled up on the couch beside him. "Turn it up."

With leaden hands, Gus passed her the remote and rose. "I'm going to bed."

As a girl Operation was Jill's favorite board game. She was fearless, tweezing her way in after the bread basket or the funny bone, anticipating with more delight than dread the sound of the nerve-singeing zap. Boldly she delved into the dark nether regions of the red plastic cavities and plucked triumphantly from the bowels of the cardboard patient the source of all his troubles. Then she knew what she was dealing with, the name of the ill and the cost of extracting it. This was something different. Something more than disappointment or nerves; something heretofore unnamed. Maybe after all these years he'd simply grown tired of taking advice from other people's dads and decided tonight to finally hold Jill responsible for it—what would a stab at that cost her? One false move, one bit of clumsy prodding, and the buzzer that guarded the perimeter of her son's broken heart would electrocute her.

Jill pressed the back of her hand against Gus's perfectly cool forehead. She pulled the covers up over his chest, said, "Tired?"

Awkwardly she knuckled his arm. "So, on the mound for game 7. Dream come true, right?" Gus rolled his eyes toward the ceiling, away from Jill, from the probe. She stuck with the obvious. "Nervous?" His answer was neither a shake nor a nod but a noncommittal quiver. "Well, it's totally normal if you are, buddy. Just try to put the nerves on hold—set them down right here—" she teased, clearing a space on his night stand. "You can pick them back up in the morning."

The Gus she knew would have smiled, said thanks mom, rolled over like a milk-drunk infant. "Is there anything you want to talk about?"

Again there was the indecipherable bobble head motion, the equivocal flux of the brow. For the first time all night it occurred to Jill that his muteness wasn't about baseball at all. He was, after all, almost twelve, the age of dark nether regions, red cavities; secrets. Maybe it was a man thing—parts growing, shifting, erupting in terrifying new ways. Or something at school. (Was it possible he'd failed all his year-end exams and was trying to muster the courage to break it to her?) Or maybe it was a girl—yes, a girl—one of those eager ponytailed softballers who'd taken to hanging around at the major games trying to distract the players and had, just this very eve, in the wake of her son's impotent swing, slipped a note through the fence and broken his heart. (Jill would string her up by her slutty little scrunchy!)

A silence like this could be almost anything. Jill could attest to that.

"Alright then," she said, rising, "Good night." With tentative steps she walked toward the door leaving between each scuff of her slippers a sonic opening for his voice. Slowly, she placed her hand on the light switch, gripped the knob.

"I love you," she said, and stepped out in the hall. In the places where the probes could never reach, the sensation of distance was palpable. It throbbed like a pulse, coursing, crashing, making grains of sand from impossible rocks. If her son did not call for her now, she would know it was time.

"Mom."

Bittersweet was the relief she felt at the sound of her own needed name. Breathing deep the shared air that lingered in their tiny hall, she girded herself and stepped back into the room. "Mhm."

In one fast burst it came, the confession, the death knell, the three most dreaded words in the lexicon of a pitching household. "My arm hurts."

Nobody panic.

Arm soreness is not necessarily a sign of negligence. A certain level of fatigue is normal at this point in the season when players have thrown balls back and forth for four long months, two practices and two games a week, and now nearly a game a day, still with the same hour-long warm-up, the same tedious, repetitive motion, again and again, back and forth, forth and back, as if perhaps they'd forgotten overnight how to throw or catch the ball and needed to reassure the coach that they still had it in them. Anyone would be sore, let alone a pitcher, who just three days before had thrown six innings, and now, in a mere four hours would be asked to do it again.

And what if he refused? If Jill refused for him. Fretfulness fueled her literary imagination as she envisioned the trail that would lead like drops of blood from such a drastic measure. It would be subtle at first, people asking almost genuinely how the arm was doing. Fathers of boys who'd waited all year for their chance would pat Gus on the back, encourage him not to overdo it. When all-star practice began the following week, he would find himself in right field; even there, his throws would we questioned, the taint of his refusal to rise to the big game casting a limp wrist on his every move. Momma's boy someone would mutter (Jill had a pretty good idea who) and that would be that; the bench would become his new home, and then, slowly (how hard is it to push someone out when they're already so close to the dugout door?) on the other side of the fence entirely. Fall ball would start but someone would forget to mention it to Gus, to Jill. His single moment of weakness would become a vortex into which his entire adolescence was sucked; by spring he'd be out of shape, out of luck. On Opening Day, he'd be skulking around the perimeter of the fence with the other castoffs, stealing away to back alleys, his baseball dreams going up in sweet, cheap smoke with losers.

Hope, gone. Future, gone. *"Oh, wretched earth engulf me!"*

Somehow it was all Rod's fault. Jill couldn't say how exactly. Only that he should have known—big, pro like him. He should have noticed if her son's throwing motion was deleterious. He should have warned her, should have helped him. Hate rose up in her belly in flames that whole bergs of ice, heaping bushels of ibuprofen, could not quell. Two can play this game, Rod Demps-

"Um, Ms. Oberdorf?"

The sight of thirty-two, able-bodied, addle-minded young adults came as something of a shock to Jill. She cleared her throat and said, "Yes?"

"You were going to tell us about next week's paper?"

"Yes. I mean, no. No paper next week. Sometimes it's best to rest the instrument a bit," she said and with that, began to load up her briefcase. The students looked quizzically at the clock, at each other, until, inexplicably, Jill said, "That's it for today."

Desks were toppled in the exodus as Jill tore out a sheet of notepaper and penned a hasty sign: **Remedial Comp 2:00 Canceled** and stuck it to the door with a piece of gum she peeled from a nearby wall. Her train of thought returned to ground zero: Gus at home alone in pain and the hazier realm of culpability. In the dusty bleachers of her mind, she could hear the calumnies building to a froth, threw her body over Gus in defense. Just because her son's arm hurt it didn't mean he'd done something wrong. Just because her son's arm hurt, it didn't mean he was fair game for pity. Just because her son's arm hurt it didn't mean he was destined to be one of the boys who'd been indomitable at twelve and by fifteen—felled by overuse and junk pitches people delighted in tsssking— was on his third surgery.

Although Jill had never before let him play hooky from school, or stay alone in the apartment for more than the time it took her to cross the street for a carton of milk, the decision had not been as hard as she'd imagined. Things were expected of her son, and, by extension, of her. She'd enlisted a neighbor to dispense a midday dose of Advil. She'd downloaded a scheduled rotation of ice and heat from the S.I. Kids website and called home between morning classes to enforce it. She'd rubbed him down with Ben-gay in the morning, and would, upon her impending arrival, do so again.

See.

Just because her son's arm hurt it didn't mean that Jill was a bad mom.

Thrown for a curve.

Jill climbed the outer steps of their apartment building as if preparing to enter the pages of some Dickensian drama. She braced herself for the sight of her son laid up on the couch hobbled, frail. Too weak to shake the ice packs he would cry out, "Oh mother," his feeble voice wrought Cockney through hardship. At the threshold of this defining moment, Jill stood unarmed. Surely, wisdom would spill forth from some unknown source and from her lips the absolute knowledge of right and wrong. Years from now Gus would recount to his wife and his own ball-playing kids how on a single afternoon in June his mother had, through clarity and vision and steel-wool resolve, made him the man he was today. Touching her hand to the door, Jill listened for a word. *Thump.* In an instant she was on the inside, the mystery made clear.

"Oh good, you're early," Gus said, glove in hand, ball in glove. "Think we can run over to the batting cages before the game?"

Jill circled him like a specter, her hand outreached as if to verify his existence in this form. Joy, relief, redemption, these alone were the things she would have expected to feel upon finding her son standing before her as if nothing was wrong—ever!—her entire day of waiting-room worry, second guessing, projections of doom, forsaken students, (had she

137

really summoned her pitching student out of another class for counsel?), all for naught. Glorious naught. Wretched naught. Jill bit her lip and asked. "How's your arm?"

With a shrug so casual whole universes of worry were cast like paper shackles in a heap, he said, "Great." Jill scrutinized his eyes, his lips, the timbre of his voice: it was the baseline reading, unbeknownst to her, by which a thousand future inquiries would be measured.

The physics of baseball.

The same moony, wandering eye that prevented Jill from keeping stats, had, over the years led her to stockpile, in that dank and fruity cellar of perception, patterns of athletic behavior that had orchestrated themselves, unwittingly, into a theory: at no time in a pitcher's life—not before, not again—was the opportunity for dominance greater than at the age of twelve. At eight or nine, new pitchers missed the strike zone as often as they hit it, and even then, at a speed that was well within the average batter's ability to catch up. But by twelve, the golden year of Little League baseball, the year for which Little League families had long squirreled away their grandiose hopes, that same 45-foot span from the mound to home plate had become for the pitchers like the climbing structures of their dying youth: child's play. The best of them could place a ball with near-surgical precision and back it up with enough power to trump the reflexes of the pre-algebra laden, geography-sopped, testosterone-flooded 12-year-old brain. Physics, neurology, stats, life wisdom they would all bare Jill out on this. And so it was, as the season came to an end, on every major field of every Little League park in America, the burden of critical games was no longer carried by the twelve boys on either team, but on the steady, thickening shoulders of two, the outcomes of championships often hinging on a single walked batter, a desperate, blindfolded whack of the bat. Ladies and gentleman, we have ourselves a pitching duel!

Dodgers vs. Yankees.

Gus vs. Zach.

Jill vs. Rod.

The game was scoreless after five innings. Jill no longer worried about Gus's arm; he had struck out ten batters already—one more than Zach—three of them in the fourth inning. His arm was fine. "C'mon Gus, one, two, three," she shouted, stalking the dry yellow grass between the bleachers like a veldt as her son walked to the mound for the top of the sixth.

To the first batter, Gus threw four straight balls, the last one high and wild. "Alright, buddy, settle down. Let's get the next one." Gus walked the second batter and the rumble began, the tremors of blood thirst gone too long unquenched. Savagely, Jill growled, "Right here, Gussy!"

The first pitch to the third Yankee batter was a strike. So, too, the second: a swing and a miss. But 0 and 2 was not an out. Neither was 1 and 2. 2 and 2. "Full count!" the umpire called. Jill doused her snatched cigarette in an old Coke cup and shouted. "C'mon, you've got this guy!" The fourth pitch was not even close enough to argue.

"Time."

A thousand heads (all right, but it was two hundred easy) turned as Gus's coach walked out of the dugout and approached the third baseline. One step across that line and Gus would be pulled. The duel would be over. It would be anyone's game. The Coach placed his sneaker on the white powder and stopped dead, waiting for Gus to come to him. He placed his hand on Gus's shoulder, formed between them a reprieve in the air.

Jill'd always wondered what manuals these men consulted. What special coursework in sports psychology they'd completed to prepare them for such crucial tête-à-têtes? Searching her own archives for inspiration—Whitman, Kipling, FDR, Dear Abby—she found there was no shortage of choices. But discernment, this was harder to come by. How was a person to know what a boy like Gus needed to hear at a moment like this? Whether to push or to coddle, to goad or encourage. It was not just the language, but the tone, the pacing, the subtext, the implication of the well-placed pause. Her lips fluttering madly, she stood on the sidelines, destiny hanging on the every word of a man whose specialty, according to the sign on his truck, was termite control.

The talk.

How d' ya feel?

Fine.

We need to hold those runners.

I know.

Just gimme some strikes.

I'm trying.

Alright then, go get 'em.

Inspired anew.

To the next batter, Gus threw three straight strikes hard and sure and as if he alone knew the inning was already in the bag. The second batter hit an easy grounder to short. It would be years before Jill understood that a hit like that was just as much a reflection of her son's pitching as the batter's hitting, but for now, she would take it. Two down. Suddenly the low-lying rumble gave way to a raucous, gasping silence as the growing crowd (men were still arriving from work, double-parking, nonchalantly running to the fence) turned to see, emerging like a bear in spring from the Yankee dugout, Zach Dempster.

According to the experts, moments like these were defined by a precise but immeasurable equation: Pitcher plus ball plus a systemic distribution of adrenaline perfectly calibrated to elevate performance without undermining control. To what extent her son's resolute faith in the power of his lucky underpants factored in, Jill was unsure.

At short, Mario repositioned the outfielders— back, back. Farther still. Zach stepped up to the plate and kicked his cleats in the dirt like a mule. He jutted out his chin and flashed a taunting smile. Like Rushmore granite, Gus set his face, unblinking, unflinching, and threw the first pitch, low and fast—faster even than the pitches he started the game with— and the first strike of the last out was recorded. Jill needed a

143

leg. She slid in next to Mr. Urbino, elbows on knees, burrowing. She made blinders of her hands, blocking out everything but the sight of her son and the ball in his hand and then, whipping right, the end result.

The second pitch was too high for a called strike. Zach swung anyway.

"What the hell are you playing? Tennis?" Rod shouted.

With her son one strike away from a shutout, Jill suddenly felt a warm and curious stillness. Particle stillness. Time marked at the speed of poured honey. As if the same gracious neurochemicals that were sustaining Gus in this moment were now working their shape-shifting magic vicariously on her, the great, green world grew macro-zoom clear. A tuft of dandelion blew past the infield and down the third base line. A single bulb in a string of bulbs that formed the numbers that flashed the scores flickered and died, leaving one of the zeros in question; Jill saw it clear as day. Heard, in the distance, the voice of Vin Scully and a crowd of cheering Dodger fans crying out from the radio of a passing car. Nothing eluded the scope of her senses.

To the mound Jill turned her keen gaze. She saw the shift in the iris of her son's eye as he lifted his leg and lunged. Like a soap bubble from a blow stick, the ball left his hand. Jill could almost trace the seams as it meandered toward the plate. It looked like a perfect strike (she only hoped that Zach could not see it coming in as well as she could), but then, the oddest

144

thing happened. As if there had been some obstruction in the air from point A to point B, the ball abruptly swooped, setting off on a new and ill-aligned course, one that would surely result in a hit batter, and a base runner, and the disgorging of the unforgiving flood. Her mouth widened in anticipation of the need for an outlet for pain, gaped wider still as the ball did something even more unlikely: veered back in line, passing lazily through the strike zone, and just below Zach's impotent, whooshing, third-strike bat.

Funny, that ball. It was almost as if it had curved.

Control.

Contrary to all the Freudian radar-gun bravado, speed was not a pitcher's primary weapon. The ability to hit his spots, to say to the ball go here and it listens; don't go there and it obeys. Control. This was the factor above all others that determined a pitcher's success. Clem had taught Jill that.

In waves, the shock of her son's side-armed rebellion hit. She wasn't sure which was worse, that he had defied her or that he had done it so brazenly, shamelessly, right out in front of God and the world as if trusting the fact that his own mother was too stupid to even recognize what he was doing. Jill didn't dare ask herself how long he'd been throwing the very ball she'd forbidden him to throw— once, twice, all season long? No one else seemed to be surprised by it.

"C'mon, Jill," someone said with a swat. "Rally caps!"

Numbly, limply, she turned her cap inside out but there would be, she knew, no rallying from this. In the two-person home Jill called her entire family, she had just lost something elemental. Recklessly, masterfully her son had usurped it from her, and staring her down sidelong as he strode off the mound, dared her to do something about it.

The box on the high shelf.

Above the mothballed stacks of winter sweaters and the board games they had planned to make a Friday night ritual of and the backdated shoe boxes of bills and receipts, an opaque plastic storage box did its best to look inconspicuous. Jill locked the door. She set the box down on the bed and with sarcophagi reverence lifted the lid. She always went for the ball first, the ball he'd given Jill the night he pitched a no-hitter. The smudges of green and red earth and something like the smell of his hand were still there. Pressing the leather to her lips, she breathed so deeply pins and needles pricked her skull.

Jill rested the ball on her pillow and continued the excavation: a copy of the official Wildcats program, ticket stubs from every game she'd every watched him play, a napkin from Pancho's, a dorm key, a dried sprig of sage she no longer recalled the import of, and a small handmade booklet entitled Jill's Personal Guide to Pitching. On index cards and glue-sticked construction paper were all of Clem's insights on the Knuckleball, the Curveball, the Slider, the Splitter, the Fastball and the Change-up. There was nothing about execution, only what Jill should learn to look for as they came across the plate. How to be a smarter fan. How to better appreciate all the things a good pitcher does. To say that it was all Greek to Jill would be unfair; Greek she could understand.

On the inside back cover, Clem had pasted a Polaroid of himself practicing his pick-off face. Jill smiled and the years, the hour, the bedtime of the son who'd resulted from their comingled flesh, fell away. She had forgotten how magnificent he was to look at. How his bare chest had inspired her not to read a single book, or write a single line, or critique the efforts of anyone but the plate ump right up until the day she'd driven off the campus, hoping, praying even (lot of good that did!), that he'd come after her.

Some of the artifacts were more current. From a manila envelope Jill withdrew a stack of clippings, the fruits of twelve years of surreptitious visits to the campus library to check the back pages of *Baseball Weekly*. The last time she'd seen his name in print was three years ago. A single sentence without compassion or grace or even the decency of prepositions. C. McGaffey, Diamondbacks, AA El Paso to AAA Tucson.

Jill had taken it as a sign. The cosmos were conspiring to bring a father closer to his son, to bring Clem back to the place where it all began, to reconcile the Act 1 conflicts of their young lives. She was, after all, only thirty-seven (not too old to start again), and Clem, his passing years scratched on her soul like tally marks on a prison wall, would, in a matter of days, (finally!) be thirty. Like a snapshot of a moment that had already transpired, she could see them together on the other side: the boys playing catch in the yard; Jill serving patio trays of fresh lemonade, ice clinking in the glasses like happy teeth.

Only the how and the when remained surreal, dreamy, fiction. So vivid were the details of her imaginings, it was unthinkable that they would never come to pass.

Faithfully, Jill had waited for a mystic nudge, a celestial *Now!* that would override the doubt and regret and the terror of the fallout of the unforgivable act that had for a dozen years immobilized her. She imagined it as an opening, a hand, a bridge; the worst—poof!—in a blink, behind her. When it came in the form of a junk ball and a glimpse of the incipient hate in a fatherless boy she almost failed to recognize it.

Beneath all the remnants of Clem was a cigar-sized box with ornate sides and a sturdy, cloth-flapped hinge. Inside, the contents were laid out like a first-day-of-school outfit and all its promises for the coming year: two tiny lead crystal bottles of ink nestled in velvet wells, an ebony-handled quill, two brass nibs, and a bundle of old-fashioned, crème-colored writing paper bound in a purple ribbon and sealed with a gold-waxed J. *To Jill from Santa* she'd written expectantly on the tag the year Gus started Kindergarten. Just as soon as she'd taught him to loosen his grip on his pencil, recite the months of the year, tell a "b" from a "d" with confidence; just as soon as they buried the goldfish, outgrown Velcro, pasted the googly-eyes on the sock puppet of Rumplestiltskin; right after President's Day, Easter, Daylight Savings; just as soon as she nit-picked his hair, washed the sheets and the blankets and the towels, taught him to snap and whistle and blow bubbles with gum;

just as soon they got him new shoes, a play date, found the right leaves for the caterpillars—crossed these few last things off her list—surely, then, a surfeit of time to write would be hers.

Dear Clem.

I know you must have met a lot of fans over the years, so I hope you still remember me. I'm the one who thought that baseball was a game played by fat, tobacco-chewing thugs until I saw my first Wildcats game. I used to proof your English papers and make you protein smoothies in the dorm kitchen (let's hear it for R.A. privileges!). The last time I saw you (has it really been twelve years?) we were toasting your future over cactus-flavored margaritas and I was promising your mom that I wouldn't distract you. (I haven't, have I?) Okay, that's all the hints you get. Anyhow, the reason I'm writing is that, believe it or not, I have a son who loves baseball. He'll be 12 next month, actually, and he's a pitcher, too. He just pitched in the championship game of his whole Little League and struck out thirteen players. Then he hit the game-winning double in the bottom of the sixth to bring in the winning run. I know I'm bragging, but he actually reminds me a lot of you. I've enclosed a picture. His name is Gus.

The reason I'm writing is that I could really use some advice from you about this whole curve ball business. I've told Gus a million times he's not allowed to throw them but his all-star coach, a supposed former pro, seems to have taught him one behind my back and now I guess he's really good at it. I'm not even sure how long he's been doing it, or if he may have already damaged his arm. I just don't know. Maybe if you could write him a letter and tell him how dangerous it is. I'll just tell him you're an old friend of mine. That would be okay, wouldn't it? I've tried to follow your career over the years. It looks like a lot of different teams have been fighting over you. I hope you're happy with the Diamondbacks and that they call you up soon. They're fools if they don't. School's out next week, so maybe if you're still there, we can fly out for a game. I know it would be a big thrill for Gus to meet a real pro. As for me, tell your mom she was right about my job being stable. I'm still here, teaching kids to write who'd rather be doing anything but. I hope one day I'll have time for my own writing again, but for now it's on the back burner. (A single mother never rests!) I so admire how you've stuck with your pursuit, Clem. Hang in there. I know you always said if you didn't make it to The Show by 30 you'd hang up your cleats, but please don't. I believe in you.

Maybe it was the hour or the wine or the fact that she'd waited twelve years to write the words, but her pen would not be stilled. Cryptically, she added in closing: *We both do.*

Happy Birthday, Clem McGaffey.

Dawn over the hills of Cortaro was a gift of sherbety air for those who woke to greet it. Gabby strode to the top of her favorite ridge with firm, jubilant steps. Lizards and woodcrests and tremulous rattlers scattered beneath her feet as she planted her walking stick in the soft earth and continued to rise. With each step the old chains of guilt and burden, of carrying the weight of men's failures like wounded soldiers on her back, fell away. In the hollow of secondhand anguish, Gabby had blossomed; beauty from nothingness, from thorniness, beauty sprung from a core-deep well of stored water.

After three years in the desert, she no longer thought about moving on. Here in the outskirts of Tucson she had, once again, adapted, survived— thrived, even— shedding old skin like a copperhead on the trail that wended through the monastic foothills and back down past the RV park where her son still insisted on living: his ability to adapt remained to be seen.

The graceful, upswept bun that had been her last vestige of more sophisticated days was now cropped short, the dove gray spikes gelled roguishly for effect. It was striking really, the way the silver streaks played off the blue of her eyes and the brown of her sun-stained skin and the pale petal pink of her scoop-necked leotard beneath which she no longer wore a bra. Eliciting stares was not the worst thing that could happen to a single woman at sixty-one.

There wasn't time to bake a cake. Gabby's morning began with back-to-back classes of biscuit-thighed, melon-tummied, diaper-clad primas whose mothers saw in them a precocious grace they felt it selfish to deny the world. Gabby smiled and cashed their checks. No sooner had the toddlers waddled out than the lean and superior kindergartners they hoped to grow into strutted through the door. Gabby drew the red velvet curtain behind them, turned up the Bach, shut out all evidence of their inconsequential, dot-in-the-wilderness existence; inside her adobe, strip-mall studio it was Vienna, St. Petersburg, New York City, the audience applauding wildly just past the lights of the wall-to-wall mirror. Stomachs in girls! At three o'clock, the serious students arrived with their out-turned feet and their pinned-back shoulders and their priggish, crochet-covered buns. Like dying swans they threw themselves into the requisite suffering of their art: the martyrdom of their bloody feet, the daily torture of their lithe and sinewy musculature, the denial of their persistent breasts. Some days they would eat no more than a single banana, breaking off bits of the sweet, starchy pulp by the hour, hoarding the rationed nibble like simians as they battled the reflection of their slovenly, corpulent mothers looking on desperately through the glass. Gabby thanked God for these homely, dependable women. They, who held her fundraisers and sewed the pageant costumes. They, who in a pinch—in the

154

hope that their servitude might translate into a bigger part for their daughters in the next performance—would run down to the corner grocery and pick up a roasted chicken and a bagged salad and a birthday cake, as needed.

There was no message on the cake, just a braid of icing and a smattering of sugary confetti. Clem blew out seven candles due to nothing more symbolic than the fact that that was how many Gabby had found in an old kitchen tin that had moved with her through the years, through homes and storage and trailers and now here to her own two-bedroom condo.

"Oh, here. Before I forget." Gabby slid an envelope across the table. "This came for you in the mail."

Gabby's new tablecloth was a sunburst of poppies. It matched the juice glasses and the oven mitts and the vase of live buds that sat with a grouping of terra-cotta-potted herbs on a window box behind the sink. Degas lithos lined the walls. Books, not trophies, filled the shelves. In all of her 900 sq. feet, the only evidence of the sport that had dominated their lives for the better part of a quarter century was a baseball cap on Clem's twelve-year-old head in a photo of him with his dad at the helm of a Mississippi riverboat, the two of them announcing in ribald shouts the depths of the muddy water, "Mark! Twain!"

With a safe and pleasant nostalgia, Gabby watched as Clem flipped over the envelope, wedged his calloused thumb beneath the flap, removed the contents. Happy 29th!!! the greeting card shouted. For a fraction of a second, the kind the near-dead report experiencing, Gabby considered the possibility that some inexplicable miscalculation—her own recent preoccupation, perhaps—had granted Clem another year of life. Reluctantly, he opened the cruel, day-glo card to the punch line. Again!

There had been no warning. No transition. Just like that, her dear, disenchanted son was expected to merrily join the ranks of all the other failed dreamers, laughing in the face of his mounting and undistinguished years. A single dollar bill fell into Clem's lap. He traced the descent, hid his face. Circling round behind him, Gabby placed her hands on his overworked shoulders. Tomorrow he would pitch for the very last time; he'll ask to keep the ball, and the ump will oblige, and the day after that, the game will go on without him.

Lifting the bill with a flourish, Clem waved it like some magnificent consolation. "Got my birthday dollar!"

Gabby laughed, considered her place in the familial ritual. "I hope I do as well remembering your kids' birthdays."

With mock ire, Clem slammed the paper-thin card shut. "Oh, so now it's grandkids plural, huh? I thought I was just on the hook for one." There were crow's feet along the corners of his eyes when he smiled, which belied, in equal measure, heartbreak and relief.

"A mother can dream," Gabby said lightly, and turned to serve the day-old cake.

Till the fat lady sings.

From the moment the sun rose the next morning there were clues that the universe was feeling magnanimous. The first was waiting for Gabby right outside her turquoise door. There, at the tip of an eye-level branch of the giant Saguaro were three green cactus fruits, ripe and plump and ready to burst. Nothing would have been more ordinary in August or September, but this was June, the time for the creamy-white blossoms that summoned the white wing doves that spread the pollen that spawned the sweet, crimson fruit that the desert dwellers—squirrels, bats, aficionados of Saguaran jellies—waited all summer for. Had she not been running late, Gabby might have noticed, but today she'd overslept. At the dawn of the day of her son's final pitching performance, she had hit the snooze button and rolled over. There was no adrenaline left to rally. In truth, she was surprised they'd kept Clem around this long; in a game where the creed is *move up or move on* a three-year stint with the same Triple-A team was an about as common as cactus fruit in June.

The clues were less subtle in the line at Cholla's cafe where Gabby stopped every morning before her first class. Everything was the same—the locals, the lattes—same as ever, and yet, somehow, there was a slowness to the air, as if the room had been suspended in a milky foam. Despite the

157

overwhelming aroma of roasting coffee, she could detect, too, the scent of damp newsprint on thumb-moistened sports pages and the faint perfume of the pale, white cactus flowers floating in a bowl by the register. The room was simply not itself. At the tottering wooden tables, where the regulars debated daily the finer points of art and religion and the pros and cons of the new Walmart, Gabby heard, rising up from the indistinguishable huzzah, her son's name, clear as day.

She ordered a decaf and threw open the door, tilting her head toward the sun to orient herself. Yes, the sky was still blue. Yes, the café table she considered her spot was still there, still empty. Their first year in Cortaro she had sat at this very seat every morning of a Sidewinders homestand, armed with schedules and coupons and always, in an official team jersey. Gabby had viewed her presence at the local hub as something of a community service. How many times had people not been quite sure of the game days, or who the opponent was, or been completely oblivious to the fact that kids got in free every third Saturday? If seeing her in an official Sidewinders jersey helped them remember that they had a minor league ball club playing major league ball right there in their own back yard and that they better go see 'em now before the good ones—the really special ones—got called up to The Show, well, that was just a win-win for everyone.

On the advice of her therapist, Gabby had stopped wearing the jersey the year she moved out of the trailer. Moved on with her life. The old Sidewinders cap she kept at all times in the outer pocket of her nylon tote didn't count. It was a sun shield, nothing more; a woman her age could not be too careful with her skin. Somewhat defensively, she slipped the cap on her head and straightened the brim till the logo faced out just so.

It was her custom to set her satchel on the second chair, but today she placed it by her feet, leaving the empty seat empty, as she settled in to what could only be described as a ready position. When an arm attached to a grabby man reached in presumptuously, she gripped the chair back like a wishbone. "No. I'm expecting someone."

This did not feel like a lie. More like a truth she was just a little fuzzy on the details of. Gabby's beloved *New York Times* remained untouched in her tote as she read instead the eyes of the passersby until the coffee was gone, the last remnant of foam licked clean. She adjusted her Sidewinders cap one last time, like a telltale carnation at a secret rendezvous, and with a deep, long-suffering breath, rescanned the horizon.

Like an eclipse he appeared, his long black robe casting Gabby in his considerable shade. She folded her arms modestly across her gossamer leotard and looked up. She had never seen one of them up close or even off the monastery grounds.

Haloed by the blinding sun, the monk spoke. "Our boys playing tonight?"

"7:00," Gabby said. The desert wind stirred without warning, brushing the hem of his garment against her bare leg. Compelled to confess, she added, "It's my son's last game."

The monk tipped his head with a fervent and unnerving curiosity. "What's his name, your son?"

Gabby could no longer feel her tongue. "Clem. Clem McGaffey."

In dimples and creases, the monk said aha!, as if Clem's name was the title of a missing chapter of a story he'd been following for a very long time. Pressing the tips of his fingers together lightly, a wry grin gave way to revelation. "I trust he has a better arm than you."

Like a child's connect-a-dot drawing, Gabby traced the beseeching balls in the desert from there to here, this moment, this man, to whom her plight, she realized with a g-force swoon, had not gone unnoticed. "Not good enough I guess."

The monk's eyes swirled and sparked like a gyroscope. "That remains to be seen."

"No, it doesn't. It's over."

The monk lay his hand on her shoulder and quoted what Gabby could only assume was Scripture. "It is inconceivable that he should perish, a son of prayers like yours."

The Bible stories Gabby knew she could count on one hand, and not quickly. Still, God's promise to Sarah, and her bearing a child at ninety flashed before her as easily as Clem's last, best ERA. But this what not the same. Sarah still wanted a child. Gabby had moved on. Gabby had put her days of living inning to inning behind her and found in that release the first liberation of her late life. "It's too late."

"Then why are you still praying?"

"I'm not. I gave up on that a long time ago."

The monk eyed the empty seat and took it. He planted his thick legs like tree trunks in the slabbed concrete, spreading them slightly to accommodate his round belly and launched into what she could only assume was a reply. "One of our brethren died last week," he said, with no particular sadness. "I was standing at his grave site. Had a perfect view of that ridge where hikers like to stop and take in the sights." The instinct to hide her face was overpowered by the need to look, to know; to be known. "Saw it clear as day. That little round blur of white, soaring through the air, dropping down in the ravine with the others. Looked just like a dove."

A single salt tear ran down Gabby's cheek. "Old habits die hard."

"Yes. I know," he said, patting his roped and rotund belly as he rose. "I've been trying to lose this for the past thirty years." Tucking in the empty chair, he shook his head. "Just can't seem to stay away from the bear claws."

Gabby wiped her eyes and snuffled, "Have you ever thought about ballet? Fifty percent off on the first ten-week session."

Like a stadium crowd tracking a ball hit deep, the

monk's laughter rose, swelled, burst. It was like a balm to her aging joints, that laugh, that sound, the fluttering wings of hope. "That's the second nicest offer I've had all day," the monk said, and stepping out across the shimmering macadam, disappeared like a mirage.

Big guns, nine o'clock.

The mind plays tricks. On the day the very thing that's been waited for a lifetime suddenly shows up on the doorstep with a dozen roses, the brain shuns it in self-defense. It leaps at nothing. Grips the psychic armrest. The neurosystem wisely douses itself with shock-inducing enzymes, preventing potential surges and blowouts. The call to step out of a wretched state and into a new and marvelous light just seems like more than anything as ordinary as a day is capable of delivering on.

Gabby's accelerator foot slackened as she eased warily into one of the reserved spots. Through a gap in the banner ads along the right field fence, she could see the men keeping watch over Clem's warm-up. They wore, in various combinations, purple pique polos and black and purple wind shirts, and, to a man, the official black cap with the snaked-logo front, gold and purple, woven into the shape of a D. Radar guns in hand, they looked liked some sort of secret service platoon, scouting everything, betraying nothing; stealth-eyes through cryptonite shades.

Gabby flipped down the car visor to check her lipstick. In the mirror she saw a little girl run past. She was wearing a jersey that read McGaffey. The Sidewinder souvenir stand sold lots of jerseys just like that (well, not as many as they used to), but this was an official McGaffey Diamondbacks jersey, and it did not exist in any store or roster or universe. Flashing a guileless smile skyward the girl ran off into the crowd, which was, Gabby noted numbly, considerably larger than usual.

Family.

The section reserved for player's families was something of a misnomer. Mainly the three front rows were occupied by a rotating band of townie girlfriends, or ex-college teammates, or divorcee dads who, having lost touch with their ball-playing sons during childhood, wanted now to reconnect. Once in a while, a real, whole family, a living, breathing, census-defying family with a mom and a dad and sons and daughters—twirling, bright-eyed, shiny-haired daughters—would fly in for a weekend in matching sweatshirts and caps and cheer as if the whole thing was all still a great, big parade in their boy's honor. After the games, Gabby was sure, the girls hopped in the back with their mom chattering brightly, putting on gloss, while in the front the dad and the player, ripe with sweat and dust, spoke in deep men's voices of minor adjustments. Oh, look, there's an Applebees someone would say, and again, everyone would cheer in unison, and off they'd go for baby back ribs, toasting their fair-haired boy's imminent success with refillable mugs raised high in the center. Even in their finest hours—maybe most especially then—Gabby's own family had always seemed like a chair with three legs, a body shy of balance.

In the first row, she took a seat beside the only person she knew by name. Marissa was the lady friend of one of the new young turks, marital status unknown. There was, however, a D-back clad toddler who came with her to each game. She wore him like a hood ornament on her sparsely covered lap. "Big guns, 9:00," Marissa said, gum cracking. "Word is they need to call up a pitcher, like, yesterday."

The Sidewinders began to emerge from the dugout. Marissa lifted the boy up over her plunging white tee and together they shook their jiggling parts in a fever cloud of support. "GO MONDO!" The excitable toddler kicked his miniature Nike cleat straight into Gabby's rib. "Ivan! Bad boy" Marissa swatted his diapered bottom, "You wanna do some kickin' we'll find you a soccer ball."

"It's fine, really," Gabby said.

"He just needs to let off some steam, that's what." Handing the toddler a bag of peanuts, she said, "Okay, little man, you go work on your throwin'."

Inches from their feet, Ivan spilt the peanuts out in an easy-to-reach pile. Lifting his knee all the way up to his pacifier, he began to hurl them, one by one, toward the fence. A nut ricocheted off the fence pole and back towards the girls. Brushing shell dust from her cheek, Gabby smiled. "He's got quite a little arm on him."

"Don't I know it." Marissa flicked her black waist-length hair back to reveal a Diamondback tattoo. "We already clocked him at 32 miles an hour the other night. Can you believe that?"

"No," Gabby said, nothing more.

"Little League says wait three more years, but they don't know shit. We're having a fake i.d. made up already. We're gonna get him drafted even younger than his daddy!"

Younger. Quicker. Faster. Anything to get the edge. What the father never had the son got by twelve, by eight. How young was too young for a 3-D analysis of a child's throwing mechanics? (Best to start 'em off right). How far could they go if only they had a batting cage in their own back yard? A machine that threw curve balls? A ball that glowed in the dark? If the big boys had it, the little boys wanted it—eye black, Under Armor, creatine—the bandwagon was crowded and the kids wanted on.

The Strike Counter in the outfield was just another example of the new-and-improved, sooner-is-better zeitgeist in sporting America. What had begun as a simple, fanspun marker and cardboard affair—a sign with the strike-out symbol "K" held up in the outfield for each earned out by the home pitcher—had quickly turned into a showy, sponsored de rigueur feature at every major, minor, and with increasing frequency, college field, in America. Gabby had watched the trend evolve, felt certain it was only a matter of time—days, weeks—before a Little League parent of a standout pitcher suggested they get one, too. You know, as a fundraiser.

At the Sidewinder Stadium in Tucson, the strike board was sponsored by the clever folks at Krispy Kreme Donuts. By the middle of the fifth inning of what Gabby felt was Clem's final game, the K-Kounter looked like this:

KKKKKKKKKKKKKKK

Returning from an extended trip to the bathroom, Marissa squealed, "Oh, my God!!" Gabby turned for a moment of shared incredulity. "You would not believe the diaper I just changed. Jesus Christ this kid can shit. So what'd I miss? Did Mondo bat already?"

"No," Gabby said. Marissa's myopia did not surprise her. Minor League baseball was not a team sport, but a showcase of individuals trying to claw their way out at any cost. Gabby was merely grateful that, in all these years, Clem had not taken up with a woman like her. There had been flings, to be sure, but nothing real, nothing lasting. No one who would ever show up at a game with a kid and proof of DNA. Turning her attention back to the field, she said, "Clem's up next."

Marissa screwed up her nose as if the scent of the diaper had followed her to the stands. "Who?"

"Clem," Gabby stated. Again. For the record. "My son. The pitcher."

An embarrassment of riches.

He didn't even look like he was trying. It was a fastball, to be sure, straight and hard and dead-bead center. Clem swatted it like a wiffle ball at a company picnic and off it flew, so high and far that each and every one of the 9,437 fans in attendance fans felt certain it had landed on the freeway and, like the apocryphal ball that had traveled a thousand miles on the roof of a train, was bound for the Cooperstown record books.

It was all too much, really. Too much for a single night to hold. Why was it that the One who orchestrated days like this was so inept at the distribution of wealth? And why was he so intractably abstruse, never clarifying whether these glorious moments were signposts of some greater moment to come, or rather, just that: great days. Precious memories. A swan song of a journey that had, without your knowledge or consent, already turned to dust and scattered itself in the wind.

Gabby had been blessed with more moments like these than most mothers got in ten lifetimes: the day Clem was chosen MVP of the 9 & 10 year-old all-stars; Clem, at 12, striking out fifteen batters in the District 25 Tournament of Champions; as a high school sophomore, hitting two home runs with an Atlanta Journal-Constitution photographer in the stands; Clem as a junior at U of A throwing a 2-hitter for a shut-out win in the championship round of the College World Series. His father, completely out of character, had pushed past an usher and run out on the field toward the center of the dog pile for what would end up being the last hug of their mutual lives.

Now, Gabby looked on as Clem trotted around third base, past the row of scouts she'd long stopped waiting for, and grew terrified. Only a child would believe that a night like this was a harbinger of a life of like nights to come. She watched Clem's teammates drag their feet from the dugout to greet him, their high fives perfunctory, distant, even cold, as if they saw in her son not a cause for celebration, but the source of some contagious failure. Overwhelmed with the sour wine sting of hot tears, Gabby cupped her hands to her face. Pressing her fingertips over the bridge of her nose, she closed her eyes and whispered like a dying wish *Please let it end like this*.

Timing.

A pitcher striking out 20 batters and going 4-for-4 with a home run is newsworthy no matter what the league. The *L.A. Times* ran a small blurb with a photo of Clem on page 4 of the Sports Section which arrived on the Oberdorf stoop at precisely 6:58 a.m. Gus was not there to hear the thud, having spent the night before at a teammate's house where they were still recounting the innings, play by play, of their championship victory earlier that week. Ordinarily, Jill would have relished the extra time to sip her coffee and read the paper uninterrupted from cover to cover, but as it was the day of the North Palms picnic, there was fruit to cut and brownies to bake and trophies to pick up on the way to the field. Juggling two lawn chairs, a cooler, a watermelon, a bag of charcoal and a giant squirt gun, Jill stepped obliviously out over the welcome mat where the folded *Times* lay like a telegram from God. By day's end, a thoughtful neighbor took the paper inside. Foolish to waste good news.

It was nearly dark by the time Jill and Gus returned home, their heads awhirl with the thrill of satin all-star jackets and deep pitching rosters and the sweet tease of the Little League World Series in Williamsport, Pennsylvania. They crossed the threshold without giving the newspaper a second thought, unaware that it had come to rest down the hall under a congealed puddle of bacon grease. Curiously, the news of Clem McGaffey's miraculous outing had been spared: clipped and saved and tacked to a cork board in apartment 3C, the flip side of a coupon for all-weather radials.

All-star math.

Of the fourteen boys selected for the North Palms 11 & 12-year-old All Star team, eight had been pitchers. Six of those had also been shortstops. They had all been starters. Not one had played a single inning in the outfield. Other than the top one or two boys, (whom most could agree on), or the bottom two or three, (whom all but the parents of those players could recognize easily), it was anyone's game. In the imaginary rosters they compiled in their minds under the pounding sun of all-star training, there was not a parent, including Jill, who did not rank their own child in the top six. The top six would start and stay. Seven through Nine would start and leave, relinquishing their spots to Ten through Fourteen, who would appear as briefly as possible. Like the quest for academic perfection that led parents to ramrod their children into the elusive and seemingly-ever-widening 95th percentile (how many kids could the top 95% hold exactly?) the assorted parents and stepparents sought to cram fourteen kids into six coveted spots. Conspiracy, not math, they all agreed, was the only explanation for a child on the bench.

The first round of all-star play was a double elimination bracket including teams from all ten leagues in the district. The North Palms All Stars took the title in just four games. Staring out at the ebullient boys as they took their victory lap around the seaside playing fields of Malibu, Jill tried to come to terms with the numbers: there had been eight teams in the majors during the regular season; eight teams times twelve players for a total of ninety-two kids; ninety-two kids times ten leagues in the district widened the pool to nine-hundred and twenty—let's call it a thousand—kids just like Gus spread out across the city with dreams of sixth-inning glory, and only one of them had gotten to be the pitcher of record for the winning team of the championship game. Only one. One in a thousand. Not since the day of her son's birth had Jill experienced awe and wonder with such humility.

"Enjoy it while you can."

The admonition came from the barrel-chested father of the player most often referred to behind his back as the fourteenth pick. His older son was a North Palms legend; he had played Division I college ball, was rumored to be headed to the Majors. "Two years from now, half these kids won't even be playing."

Jill felt like one of Socrates' cave people. The best team in the entire district suddenly revealed as nothing more than a shadow on the wall. "How can that be?"

"Some'll lose interest. Some just won't grow enough. Some are as good now as they'll ever get."

"But half?" Nothing stupefied like the numbers.

"A few of these kids will play in high school. Some'll make the team, but won't make grades. Maybe one'll go on to play in college."

Maybe one. One in a thousand.

Like ducks in a skeet booth, the boys were aligned in two neat rows, the shorter ones kneeling, the taller ones in the back. Jill scrutinized their faces, their shoulders, the jut of their chins. If there was a tell, where would it be? In their eyes? Their stance? A certain ineffable cock of the hip? Responding to a shout of *We're number one!*, the boys lifted their index fingers heavenward. As if on command, a cloud passed overhead and the sun burst forth across the field bathing the green of the grass and the white of the uniforms and the tan of the boy's sweaty, sun-kissed cheeks in golden light. On a single beam of ochre, a gull swooped into frame. It did not pass or return to the sea, but circled the lineup of boys, searching for just the right shoulder.

If all was right with the world, Jill knew from her Sunday School coloring sheets, the bird should stop just above Gus's head. Transfiguring currents would shoot out wildly in all directions and a voice would intone from the skies something about him being the One. Instinctively, she lifted the camera to her face; why she considered the alighting of birds more reliable than stats she could not say, but holding the viewfinder steady, she waited for the whitish, dovish gull to appear directly over Gus' head—now!—and snapped her last shot.

The anointing was memorialized in a 4x6 Twin-Pic

affixed to the Oberdorf's beige refrigerator. In the back-row gap between the heads and shoulders of Gus and Mario Urbino, the gull could be detected hovering in the V of dusk-tinged sky. Technically, the bird was no closer to one boy than the other, but the beak—the arrow, the messenger's instrument—was clearly pointing towards Gus's ear. Over time, Jill would come to forget her choreographic role in the shot entirely, gazing at the photo in uncertain moments, like a prophecy.

Paternity.

With each all-star victory the North Palms parents coalesced. They dressed in matching NPLL t-shirts and caps. They shared sunflower seeds and lawn chairs and pitchers of discreet margaritas. It no longer seemed to matter that they had spent the better part of the season suspecting each other of nefarious deeds—line-up fixing, draft-stacking—they were now all on the same side, the fate of their summer vacations linked by the stamina and fortitude of their gum-chewing, preadolescent sons.

"Just a few quick announcements, parents," Bev said. Rather than grow tired of the duties of a team mom, she seemed to be forging something of a career of it. "I've gotten some estimates for custom seat cushions and stadium blankets. There's a small additional fee if you want to have your child's name and number embroidered on them as well. I'll just pass these around, see if we want to place an order. Naturally, we need to take one game at a time, but as some of you know, from here we go straight to the sectionals, and if we win there, it's on to the Divisionals in Lancaster. I've found a very nice Motel 6 there that's holding twelve rooms for our team—" Bev coiled her two fingers together in a fervent wish and said, "Just in case."

Charlie Zampolli's mom confided lightly. "Oh God, I

hope it doesn't come to that. We've got a family reunion in Hawaii."

No one laughed. Her fellow all-star parents did offer several suggestions ranging from canceling the trip to keeping Charlie with them for the duration of the summer. At some point in the helpful exchange, the mother of the player who subbed in for Charlie at second base slipped away from the circle, sidestepped over to the dugout where the coaches were packing up the gear, lowered her voice.

"One more thing," Bev said, pulling out an envelope. "I have all of your birth certificates here. Let me give them back to you. But, keep them handy. There's another set of certifications at the Regional level. Here you go," she said passing one to Charlie's mom, and Tucker's Dad and, "Oo, what a pretty color," she said as she handed over the birth record of Mario Urbino.

Passing the next one to Jill she offered a tight smile. "And this one is yours."

Like a fig leaf, Jill put her hand over the line where beneath the word Father it read: unknown. Twelve years before, in the aftermath of labor, it had seemed no more binding than an election-poll response of undecided.

Slide!!!!!

The Loser's Bracket was dirty business. With their backs against the wall after a one-run loss in the opening game of the Sectionals, the North Palms all-stars dove and slid and dogsled barbarously after each impossible, stay-alive victory. Night after night after nail-biting night, Jill measured their progress in quarters and detergent scoops, dousing the stains, shaking the static from the polyester pants (she'd run out of dryer sheets two days ago), wrestling the bulbous rubber cup into the absurdly narrow slit of his nylon sliding shorts (had the makers of the sliding shorts ever actually seen the shape of an athletic cup?).

From the cubby of the warm dryer, Jill withdrew Gus's crisp, white all-star jersey. The fabric was twice as heavy as the one he'd had during the regular season. It had buttons from top to bottom and cursive lettering embroidered on an angle across the center just like the pros. The dad of the fourteenth pick told Jill his older boy had worn the same number when he was 12: that was the year the North Palms All Stars had gone as far as the State championship.

Jill breathed deep the warm, linty smell and considered the cost of going all the way, of spending every single day from now until the middle of August watching ball games and washing clothes, on ever-distant fields, in ever-distant

Laundromats, making ever more inane chatter with strangers upon whom a certain intimacy had been thrust; like inmates counting the minutes till their next shift in the yard, so, too, the all-star parents would kill the hours from game to game restraining, with varying degrees of success, vainglory, dyspepsia, festering, and increasingly violent, impulses, as they journeyed to the promised land of Williamsport, PA. Jill smoothed the thick, venerable blue letters and patted them twice for luck. With a twangy, unmelodic hum, she smothered the urge to get ahead of herself, and hoisting the basket up the stairs, vowed to take it one wash load at a time.

Did you catch the mustache on that kid?

At the Sectional level of play, size was everything. Even in the parking lot. There was not a vehicle that seated less than an infield, and each of them spray painted like Christmas retail displays with the names and numbers of the players on the teams which had grown confident with their round-1 wins and were now starry-eyed with nationally-televised glory. Rumors flew like corked-bat homers that Fox SportsWest might be covering some of the early tournaments on the Road to Williamsport. Everyone knew that a shot of the pitcher's mom was, along with the jazzy ads for beer and Viagra, a staple of that sort of coverage. Jill ran a brush through her hair, checked her lipstick, slipped into the dank and dimly lit stall of the bathroom to pee. Again.

"Well, I know a woman who works with a mom who lives in South Beach," a familiar voice claimed upon entering. "She says they put something in the water— amino acids or something. Every kid in the town looks like that."

"Omigod, did you see that number 4. I'm telling you that kid has an Adam's apple bigger than my husband's."

By the leaking sink, theories abounded about North Palms' first-round competition. "I heard they've been recruiting from out of the district."

"I heard that they've had the whole team working

during the off-season with a boot camp drill sergeant."

"I heard that number 22 is really one of the nanny's kids. He doesn't even live here. They just brought him up for the season."

"Probably drove here himself."

Jill held her head between her knees. Her nose filled with the smell of urine and damp concrete. Beneath her thighs, the thump, thump, thump of her thwarted blood flow threatened to topple her. In the pin-prickly spin of her head the familiar voices continued. Voices of women who, just the day before, she had held hands with in the shared sisterhood of 6th-inning anxiety.

"Well, let's just hope Gus'll be able to hold 'em."

There was a sortof mulchy silence, like the wads of wet toilet paper stuffed in the mysterious cracks in the tile.

"He does have that curve ball."

"Larry says it's not even very good, it's just our boys aren't used to seeing pitches like that."

"Well they shouldn't be. Twelve-year olds should stick to fast balls, that's what Frank says."

"I can't believe she lets him throw it." This from Bev, who just the day before had suggested adjoining rooms at the Motel 6. "You know he's going to blow his arm out."

"Well, what do you expect with no dad around?"

"Has anyone ever met Gus's father?"

"She doesn't even know who he is!"

"What?!"

"That's what it says on the birth certificate," Bev said, lowering her voice to an officious whisper. "Don't tell anyone I told you."

Jill braced herself against the graffitied door. She waited for the voices to fade from the room, from her ears, from the scorched nodes of her memory. In the distance she could hear a warbled recording of The Star-Spangled Banner. Alone in that forsaken stall, it seemed to her something of a hymn. Her head bent as if on cue. Placing her hands together she touched the tip of her nose with her fingertips and held so still whole volumes were written in the silence.

...oh, say does that star-spangled

banner yet wave,

o'er the land of the free,

and the home of the brave.

Jill longed for another verse, but it was not to be. The relative comfort of pre-game limbo came with the cry of "Play Ball!" to an abrupt and bracing end. Jill leapt to her feet. She doused her face with rust-tinged water. She blotted it with a coarse, brown towel. Burying her eyes beneath the visor of her new Proud North Palms Parent cap, she freshened her lipstick with a defiant pucker, and headed out.

The noise was unlike anything she'd ever heard. Savage. Ghastly. Like slack-leashed pit bulls, the rival players clawed at the dugout fence, yapping, whooping, snarling, hissing. Somehow there was already a South Beach base runner on first and another at the plate. Gus threw Ball 2 and the vicious hectoring swelled: primal, flesh-dripping yelps that had no other goal than to rattle her beloved son. Throwing herself against the fence, Jill cried, "Hey blue. They can't shout like that can they?"

The umpire turned, shrugged. "Up to the coach to complain."

The second batter spread his legs across the chalked box. "C'mon Gussy, find your pitch!"

Gus lifted his leg. Marshaled his torque. Hurled the ball in the air. Like a bag of nuts from a stadium vendor, it came across the plate for an easy line drive to right field. A minute and a half into the game and already there were runners on first and second. *AYY-YI-YJ!! Step right up! A YY-IE- Owza-Ay! Get your meatballs right here!*

Jill turned toward the North Palms dugout for signs of Rod emerging from the shadowy tarp in Gus's defense. She could see, from this angle, the point of his bent elbow, his crossed arms, the glint off his wraparound shades; never had a body given off less of a sense of imminent movement. With a desperate lunge, she approached the woman selling raffle tickets. She of the host field. She of the universal maternal bond of love and equity. "Someone's got to tell those kids that this is unacceptable!" Jill insisted.

"Should have been here yesterday," the raffle lady

replied. Reaching her fingers up to her ears, she withdrew two sponge plugs. "This is nothing."

Batter number three, the one with the lip hair and the Adam's apple and the cup that seemed to stand up at attention, stepped into the box. *AA-II—EE-AY!!!* He leaned in so close to the plate, there was no way for the ball not to hit him.

"Ouch!" the commentator said into the microphone. "Now, there's a young man who knows how to take one for the team."

"And with no outs in the top of the first," the second man added colorfully. "South Beach has loaded the bases."

The clamor from the South Beach dugout grew so frenzied, Gus lifted his hand to the ump for time. Jill watched as her son circled the mound, crouched down, rubbed his hands against the dirt. She considered making a hasty sign to hold up at the fence: Remember David and Goliath. But then remembered she'd forgotten to teach him the story.

"Well, if this is the kind of sportsmanship we're going to be seeing at the next level," Jill said addressing no one in particular, "You can just count me out."

The eyes that dared to meet hers looked blankly away. Even Mario Urbino's father had been lost to her, sitting now, in the center of a circle of family—cousins and aunts and grandfathers and babies—huddled together like a merry display of nesting dolls. The human psyche wasn't built to endure suffering like this alone. Sitting at the far edge of the lowest plank, Jill was considering the companionship of a neutral party: the sno-cone vendor, say, or the old man from the local Elks lodge that'd sponsored the tournament pins.

And then, like a current, a warm body descended the planks and settled in beside her. "It's still early," Tucker's mom said. Up until that moment the only real thing Jill knew about her was that she often waited outside the dugout with her son's inhaler.

"They're just so big," Jill replied.

"They do seem to be, don't they?"

Tilting a plastic pouch in Jill's direction, she offered, "Seeds?" And together they chewed and spat as Gus walked the next batter, and the next, walking in the first two runs and leaving the bases loaded still. Where once there were encouraging shouts of "let's get this next one," or "bring it down, Gus," or "just play catch" now there was nothing. The silence emanating from her own stands was more agonizing than the zoo-frenzy from across the field.

"Right here, right now, Gussy!"

"Here we go, North Palms!" Tucker's mom added supportively.

But the only real encouragement seemed to come in the form of the sight of Rod emerging from the North Palms dugout. The silence was quickly replaced by the whirr of gears turning in rampant speculation as the parents tracked the alpha-manager's wide, dismounted-horse strides. Squirrelishly, Jill held the wad of pulpy seed casings in her cheek as Rod took his slow, purposeful steps toward the infield. When, at the third baseline he stopped short, placed a hand on Gus's shoulder in a way that could almost be construed as compassionate, the groaning was audible. Jill pretended not to hear the variations on the theme that if only her son was physically removed from the mound this instant, life as they knew it would get markedly better. Tilting her head ever so slightly in Tucker's mom's direction (was her name Sue?) she said, without eye contact, "I feel like everyone hates me."

"Temporary insanity," Sue said, patting Jill's knee.

"You know, he's not even twelve yet."

"Your son's a great player."

"Thank you." Reaching for a tissue and a single memory of anything Tucker had done to contribute, Jill sniffed. "Your son is too."

Rod swatted Gus on the butt and returned to the dugout. Jill tried to read her son's shoulders, his eyes, his stride. The talk seemed to have done him good. He circled the mound, bent down in the dirt, fanned his hand across it as if it were owned acreage. When he stood back up, Jill swore he looked taller.

"It's only two runs," she said, a believer once again.

"C'mon North Palms!" Sue shouted, "Let's have some fun out there!! "

Like a pitcher who knew a called strike was on the

other end, Gus went into his wind-up. Jill could not tell if it was a curve ball or a fast ball or a four-fingered flamingo; all she knew was that two seconds after it left his hand it was flying off the bat like a pinball hit to a 10,000 point hole and straight over the fence. A grand slam for a six-run lead. Rod came back out, crossed over the line, waved Zach over from first, and took the ball from Gus's hand. Jill was embarrassed to admit she felt more relief than disappointment.

The score was 9-0 before Zach and the team were able to get themselves out of the inning. Any attempt to rally was quickly thwarted by the towering South Beach pitcher.

"There's no way that boy is twelve."

"I heard he's been clocked at 92 miles per hour."

"Well I saw him changing in the parking lot and I'm telling you he had back acne—so, you tell me."

Zach returned to the mound in the second. It took him forty pitches to get two outs. Mario was called in to finish off the inning and, three North Palms pop-outs later, was right back at it, struggling, laboring, giving up four runs before he, too, was pulled. Bev's son, Ryan, was able to shut down the third, but shortly thereafter, batting seventh, failed to conceal his contempt for the ump's third strike call and was thrown out of the game, leaving the fourth inning pitching duties to the backup right fielder and the starting catcher, who did no worse than anyone else. Hope did make a minor appearance, when, in the bottom of the fourth, Gus hit a hard line drive past the third baseman for a double, but the thrill was not ultimately reflected in the score.

"Omigosh!" Sue grabbed Jill's arm as the last pitcher was revealed. Tucker, by his mother's own admission, had not pitched an inning since the minors; he was too gangly to throw the sort of heat required at this level; his asthma, she said, holding her hand over her heart, tended to flare up under stress. Nonetheless, with slow, deep breaths and a pitch so lumpish it utterly confounded the power-hitting South Beach team, the wheezy and unspectacular player managed to earn for North Palms and himself the dignity of three straight strikeouts, the most celebrated event in the whole miserable game.

And so it was the North Palms all-star season ended. They would not be going to Lancaster or Williamsport or The White House. Gus would not get to tell the ESPN commentators that his favorite subjects were Math and P.E., that his hero was Curt Schilling. Jill would not be asked in the stands how she handled the pitcher's mom jitters. They would not even be staying four to a room in the Motel 6, hanging socks on the clothes line they'd strung across the shower while they waited for the pizza to come. Moments after the fifth-inning mercy score of 27-0, the thick, white jerseys were stripped from the children's backs, while their parents were left to shuffle and mutter and cling to tenuous alliances, uncertain now of how to fill the summer days they'd left wide open, just in case.

Manna from Fed-ex.

Of course, over the past four weeks the question of Clem had intermittently needled. It was conceivable, Jill supposed, that he never got the letter. That the address was wrong or the mail sorter was slow or that a laser-printed autographed photo was, in adherence to Sidewinder policy, presently en route bulk rate. These were the more sanguine possibilities. Less heartening were the scenarios in which Clem had already read the letter and had simply chosen not to respond. That Jill had never been that important to him. That his life had been littered with missives from ex-girlfriends with sons who needed guidance in pitch selection. That he hadn't fully comprehended the significance of her particular message, or worse, that he had. Jill had taught him well to read between the lines. Was it really so unlikely (she had hardly been subtle) that he had understood her revelation perfectly? That by some narrow and misguided interpretation he had somehow twisted the history of their mutual lives in a way that made Jill the bad guy? That even as the delicious, wholesome, frozen lasagna she had prepared lovingly for their son was filling the apartment with its comforting steam, he was fast engaging the services of some ruthless attorney? Or (and this was easier to picture) that Gabby was?

In a blink, summer and all its chances would be over.

190

Jill could not afford to sit idly by until the hard truth of fathers and sons reappeared like an obelisk in their living room. She would not wait for the news to be sprung by a knock on the door and an indecorously served subpoena. Over cheesy slabs of Stouffer's, she held her breath and dove. "So, I've been thinking," she said in a lilt unnatural enough to lift Gus's brow. "Your birthday's coming up next week..."

"Yeah," Gus said, running a chunk of bread through the sauce. "I think I just want to go to the beach."

"Oh."

"No big deal or anything. Just some of the guys. Maybe get one of those giant subs. Okay?"

"Well, sure. We can do that..." Jill said, and left enough ellipses at the end of her thought to line a highway.

"Gee, mom, try not to sound so excited."

"Well, no, it's fine. If that's what you want. I guess I just had something a little more special in mind, that's all."

"Like what?"

"Oh, I don't know. Maybe take a little trip." Jill pushed the lettuce around in her bowl, touched her fork to the bottom, tapped down as if marking the spot on a map. "Maybe to Arizona."

"Arizona? What for?"

California kids never saw the merits in going anywhere else. "Well, an old friend of mine, actually, from college, is playing baseball out there, believe it or not. AAA," she said.

Jill looked up to gauge his response. Gus still seemed to be waiting for the part that had to do with him. "So, anyhow, I just thought it would be fun to fly out there for a few days, stay in a hotel, go to some games. I'm sure he'd love to meet you."

Gus took a swig of Coke and said, "Nah, I don't think so. I kinda want to take a break from baseball for a while."

Jill found his attitude admirable, healthy. Unfortunately she'd made no contingency plan for disinterest. "Well, we're just going to watch. I don't think that would be too taxing." She debated defining the word, but Gus seemed to be able to make a decision without it.

"I really just want to hang for a while. Thanks anyway." With a conciliatory wave of his fork, he offered, "Maybe next year he'll get called up, your friend. Then we could go see him at B.O.B. " Gus was waiting for her to say Bob, who? but Jill knew all about Bank One Ballpark. The *Phoenix Sun Times* had featured a daily column on the construction of the ambitious indoor/outdoor facility that would become the home to the Arizona Diamondbacks; she and Clem had read about it each morning in bed over bagels and kefir.

In a tone too stern for the conversation her son thought they were having, she replied, "Or maybe he'll get released. And we'll miss the chance to see him at all."

Gus shrugged and asked for seconds. She would just have to tell him. There was no other way. Just come right out and say it. Say, Gus—

There was a knock on the door. It was a man's hand, heavy and insistent, so heavy and insistent, in fact, that Gus's next helping flipped clear off Jill's spatula in response. "Don't answer that!"

"Why not?" Gus said as he leapt from his chair.

"Because we're eating," Jill said, blindly finagling the spilt serving from the cracks in the stovetop.

She could see him through the open doorway, the man from apartment 3C. He was holding a very large box. "This came for you earlier today."

So large was the package, Jill could scarcely see Gus's eyes as he carried it across the room. He set it down on the end of the table where no one ever sat and with Christmas-morning glee began to rip back the tape.

"Wait a minute, Gussy, who's it for?" Jill asked, wiping the sauce from her hands on a kitchen rag.

"It's for me!!!"

Like a courtroom gavel, Jill's heart began to pound as she watched Gus throw back the flaps and withdraw, in fast succession, all things black and purple and emblazoned with the logo she'd come to recognize over the years as that of the Arizona Diamondbacks: a pennant and a mug and a shot glass; a mouse pad and a key chain and a real rubber snake. Gus slipped a Diamondbacks cap on his head and crowed, "Cool!" and bent back down over the box for more. Playing cards and a soda sleeve and a little purple stuffed coyote. A license plate

193

and giant foam finger and an envelope which he tossed promptly to Jill. "Here," he said and reached down for the last item: a real, live Major League Diamondbacks jersey. Flipping it from front to back, he read the name.

"Is this your friend? McGaffey?"

Gus turned the jersey back around. Jill lifted her hand to the raised letters, ran her fingertips across them like a lover's furrowed brow.

"Mom? What is it? Don't cry. We'll go. We'll go to Arizona and see your friend, okay? That sounds great. Really."

Jill handed back the jersey and said, "He's not my friend, Gus."

"Then why did he send me all this stuff?"

She was supposed to instruct him to sit down. People were always told to sit down before receiving shocking news. Jill suspected it was less a matter of fainting and more of buying time before pulling the lever that would throw open the irreversible floodgates. "Clem McGaffey," she began, feeling each letter as it passed over her tongue, "Is your father."

And still the world spun.

Jill had expected the news to sound like a car crash, but found instead that the words washed over the room like creek water in September, clear and smooth and warm over the mossy pebbles. There were no tears. No broken dishes.

Gus surveyed the new landscape like a straight man in a poker game and said simply, to clarify. "My real father?"

194

"Yes."

There was a softening to his face, something akin to a smile, as calmly, wordlessly, he placed the items one by one back in the box and lifted the bounty up in his arms. "You mean that the two of you had sex and made me. That kind of dad?"

"Yes," Jill said.

She watched his face as he reconciled the horrific notion of his mother in coitus with the unadulterated bliss of knowing that his passion was in fact his birthright. With a curt nod, he indicated he had all the details he needed and went to his room and closed the door. Left with nothing but the envelope in her hand, on which her name was penned in delicate cursive, Jill slid her thumb beneath the wax-sealed G.

Dear Jill—

Clem and I were so happy to hear from you, and especially about your son, Gus. He sounds like a wonderful boy. In fact, he looks so much like Clem at this age I thought you'd get a kick out of seeing one of his 12-year-old photos. The reason that I'm the one writing is that Clem, believe it or not, has finally been called up to The Show. He left quite suddenly and didn't have time to write you a proper letter himself. He made me promise to contact you and send along a few goodies for Gus in the meantime. I would have sent everything sooner but we were waiting for the personalized jerseys to come in—Clem especially wanted you to have one.

As of this writing, he has not actually seen any playing time, but, as I'm sure you recall from your days of watching him, you never know when you might get the nod. I'm enclosing the Diamondbacks schedule in case you have a chance to come out for a game.

I would also like to say that I feel I owe you an apology. Over the years I've come to realize that, perhaps, I was too fanatical in my desire to support Clem in his dream. I believe I might have been particularly harsh at that Thanksgiving meal we all shared that one year; if I have made your life more difficult in any way through my own maternal zeal, I sincerely apologize. I can only hope that as a mother of a ballplayer yourself you will understand, and I hope, in time, forgive me.

I do hope you and Gus will be able to come out to Arizona for a game sometime soon. You are welcome to stay with me. I have an extra bedroom that I wish to fill one day with visiting grandkids, but as Clem has never married (he's hardly had more than a few passing dates since he left campus) the room is always empty. You would be doing a fellow pitcher's mom a great favor by sharing your son with us.

With love and regret,
Gabby

When Jill looked up from the letter, Gus was standing at attention with a duffel bag at his side. In his father's souvenir jersey, which hung down to his knees, he crossed the room to the kitchen counter, pulled a tissue from the box, handed it to his weeping mother, and, as if there was nothing further to discuss, said, "Let's go."

Dear BOB.

It was all Jill could do to convince Gus to wait until morning, the first flight out, 6:00 am. As it was, he slept on the couch fully clothed, his head on the armrest nearest the door. Now looking up from his free in-flight copy of *USA Today*, he grinned. "They used two of their best middle relievers yesterday. Dad's gonna pitch today, I just know it."

The ease with which he'd adopted the word dad was unnerving. "I don't know buddy. I don't want you to get your hopes up. His mother said they haven't quite worked him into the rotation just yet."

Gus crisped his paper and turned away. "He's going to pitch today, you just wait."

Phoenix looked smaller than Jill remembered it. The desert seemed to crawl right up to the fringes, where building block homes with Colorform pools aligned themselves in neat rows that led to the city, where B.O.B now stood like some erector-set Neanderthal in the center of the warehouse district. The key was the retractable roof, a must in a city where blistering heat and impulsive rain vied daily for attention. East Coast sports fans, with their zero-below parkas and their thermoses of brandied cider, seemed to revel in such creature discomforts, as if by their suffering they might make their home teams worthy. But this was the west; the new west, where wise men outsmarted suffering daily and lived to retire early on it.

"There it is," Jill said, pointing across Gus's lap.

Gus pressed his face to the window and knocked unabashedly as if he believed someone might actually hear him and look up.

Grand slam.

They checked in early at the Holiday Inn and headed down the street for breakfast. On the corner a workman on a high ladder was securing one end of a new banner above the crosswalk. Jill and Gus ducked beneath the sagging vinyl sign until, with a final tug from the other side, it grew taut, rising up over their bent heads with the news of the day.

Congratulations West Phoenix All-Star Sectional Champions! Good luck at Divisionals!

"Hey, look," Gus said, wide-eyed.

"I don't know about you, but I for one am glad to have our summer back." Jill crooked her arm in his and, leaving the baked kiln air of the downtown streets behind, stepped into the air-conditioned restaurant for relief.

"Welcome to Denny's," the hostess chimed. "Like to help send our boys to Williamsport?" A fluttery samba of bills and change rang out as she shook the decorated coffee can. "We're only two rounds away from the Little League World Series."

Jill looked past her toward the section of tables nearest the window and said cooly, "A lot can happen in two rounds."

The hostess pulled the menus from the slat and led them to the corner booth, her head turned around and back like a robin, preening. "I keep thinking they're going to be eliminated any minute now, but they just keep on winning."

"Actually, we've just been through it ourselves. Just went out two days ago back in L.A."

Apparently the hostess misunderstood, thought Jill had said *but enough about me*. "Listen to my voice, I can hardly speak. I'd take the week off if I could but I need to save up for the trip." Setting the coffee can down in the center of the table, she reached for her pad. "We're a little short staffed today. What can I get you two to drink?"

Continuing in the spirit of maternal non sequiturs, Jill said, "We're going to see the Diamondbacks this afternoon. His father's one of the pitchers."

"Really?" the waitress said, her mouth gaped as if to allow a new subject to enter. "Well I'll tell you, it wouldn't surprise me if Roy ended up there one day. I mean really, it's the darndest thing. He never even played baseball before this year, but the doctor told him he was getting too fat so I said, that's that, you're going to play something and it wasn't going to be basketball cause he'd probably have a heart attack, and they don't have any football out here for kids his age, and well, it was January, so I signed him up for Little League. Turns out he can whack that ball like it was nothing. Pitches pretty good, too. No one even taught him how. He just throws it straight and hard and down they go." Catching her breath, she poised her pencil for an order but did not pause to take it. "People keep saying that it's some big art form or something, but he just does it; whoosh, boom. It must just be a gift. That's what everyone says. Gift from God."

Jill closed her menu and smiled tightly. "My son's a pitcher, too. Averaged 13 strikeouts a game for the regular season. Batted .336 through the play-offs with 3 home runs."

Gus peered out from over the top of his menu to protest. "Mo-om."

But Jill would not be robbed of her coup de gras. "He pitched the entire six innings of the championship game of the whole District all-stars."

The waitress smiled as if licking her chops. "Roy was the pitcher for the championship game of the whole Section. Shut 'em out last night, 26 to nothing."

Like a pinprick to a balloon, Jill's voice lost everything. "Southern California is a very competitive area."

"Can we just eat please?" Gus begged.

"Why sure, hun. Listen to your mom and me goin' on like a coupla old hens while you're sitting here starving. So what'll you have?"

Opting not to refer to the famous breakfast special by name, Gus pointed to the picture at the top of the page. "I'll have this. With two eggs, and a short stack and a side of bacon, please."

"Gotta put some meat on those bones for next season, right?" the waitress said with a wink.

"Actually," Jill cut in, "Baseball is more of a nimble

man's game."

"Really?" The waitress withdrew her coffee can like a plate of proffered sweets. "Well me and Roy'll have to give that some thought on the plane to Pennsylvania."

Tickets, please.

The two o'clock start time was still hours away when the fans began to arrive at BOB. Some came for the batting practice, some for the beer; some just had no where else to be on a Sunday morning. Inside the dome, which was sealed to allow the stadium to cool, they knew they could find kindred spirits and a seat with their name on it. By the time Jill and Gus had finished their eggs and raced the three blocks to the stadium, it was nearly noon.

Jill stepped up to the ticket window.

"The name is McGaffey," Gus said, circumventing her. "Gus McGaffey. There should be some seats for us in the family section."

Pretty soon it would be as if she'd never existed at all. "Umm, actually," Jill said, craning around her son like a gooseneck lamp, "I don't think there are. We'll just take whatever you have left."

Gus reasserted himself "Can you check anyway, please?"

"Gus, he doesn't even know we're coming."

Still at an age where magic and logistics are believed to effortlessly coincide, he said, "So?"

"Here we are...." The ticket vendor withdrew an envelope from a file box. "G. McGaffey." Gus's eyes went wide as a pop fly—"Oh, no, wait"—that dropped unceremoniously between three racing fielders. "This is for a Gabby McGaffey. Is that you, ma'am?"

The thought of a ticket waiting in Clem's mother's name made Jill feel suddenly unworthy. Jill had not been the one to stand by his side day after day, year after year, game after endless, fruitless game, watching; waiting. Who was she to breeze in now for free seats in air-conditioned comfort? "No."

"Ya mean he's got another wife?" Gus barked. Jill had not seen his face register this level of incredulity since the called third strike in his game 6 play-off.

"Gabby is Clem's mother. Actually, she's the one who sent you all the goodies."

"Oh," Gus said, quick to make the requisite adjustment. "Then let's go sit with her."

The man shook his head, revealing a long, pink scar on his cheek. "Sorry," he said, holding up the envelope, "There's only one ticket here."

"That's okay. Just give us whatever you have. Best available," Jill rephrased, pleased to have summoned the official ballpark lexicon. Eyeing her crestfallen son, she specified further.

"Something near the pitcher's lounge."

Gus smited his forehead and looked to the ticket man for sympathy. "The bullpen, mom. It's called the bullpen."

The man winked at Gus and fanned two tickets. "Last

two in the house."

Shoving a $20 quickly through the slot, Jill said, "Are you serious?"

"Yep. The game is now officially sold out."

Jill saw it as a sign. That she was doing the right thing. That they had chosen the perfect moment. That today was, in fact, The Day.

With a teasing elbow to his mother's ribs, Gus offered an alternate interpretation. "See," he said with a victorious grin. "I told you you didn't have time for another cup of coffee."

Do you see what I see?

By the second inning it was apparent that one pair of binoculars was not going to be enough. Jill rented a second pair, and together they sat perched like bird watchers on their own distinct field studies two rows from the top of the High Pavilion. Gus's interests in the game were broad. He panned his glasses from point to point: from the bullpen to the family section to the batter to the mound and back again.

Not Jill. Jill found her mark and locked down, tracking Clem's every move in the shadows of the inner room where the pitchers waited for The Call. Even from this distance, even after all these years, the tilt of his head was as familiar to her as her own ten, crumpled toes. His cleats were propped up on the ledge of the picture window that overlooked the field, his pants pulled up at the knee, old-school style. The mystery of those glaring purple socks teased a smile from her lips; how could a thing like that, like the way a man wore his socks, be handed down telepathically? It was this she was pondering when a ripple of movement began to travel through the row of restless, pent-up pitchers like a passed note—shoulder to elbow, elbow to rib, rib to thigh— a current of mundane laughter, magnified three hundred times, that lit up Clem's face with a thousand volt smile. Even from afar, it warmed Jill's disenfranchised heart like ball leather in a player's hand.

"Is that her?"

Gus's question hit in waves: first the jarring intrusion of sound, then the shocking realization that there was someone else in the stadium— that it was a boy, her son, their son. It was all coming back to her. Jill aligned her binoculars with Gus's and asked, "Where?"

Gabby was seated in the second row above the Arizona dugout, two empty seats in from the aisle. The hard lines of the woman Jill remembered were nowhere to be seen. Beneath a pert tousle of silver hair, she looked about as intimidating as a Hershey's kiss. Forgetting momentarily that she was not actually related to her, Jill was encouraged to see that she'd aged so well.

"Yes, that's her. That's Gabby. Your grandmother."

"She looks nice."

Swerving her binoculars back towards the bullpen, Jill offered the only reply that, in retrospect, seemed fair. "It's been a very, long time."

Sweet relief.

In the top of the third inning, the Arizona ace walked two, hit one, and was down in the count on the cleanup hitter, the worst statistical outing of his professional career. Gus was ecstatic. The conditions could not have been more perfect. The D-backs would need relief, and lots of it. Turning to the bare-chested beer drinkers behind him, he entered effortlessly into the grand fraternity of bleacher bums. "They're going to bring in McGaffey," Gus pipped. "You just watch."

In the middle of the fourth, two pitchers were ordered to warm up. The men unzipped their jackets, laid them on the bench, took their spots on the narrow strip of Astroturf to throw. "It's too early to bring him in," Gus said, assuring his mother, himself. "You never bring in your key relievers this early."

Jill panned the field for a second opinion. Everything she needed to know would be on the face of the pitcher's mom, but the seat that Gabby had occupied only moments before was now empty.

Are you sure?

Out on the concourse, four innings into a sold-out game, there was no ticket line to speak of. The delay, which was slight, was for a change in shift. Gabby waited patiently as the ticket man with the scar on his cheek stepped out of the booth, and a small, round Latina hopped up on the stool.

"I left some tickets here for my friends—"

The fact of them—of Gus and Jill—still caught in her throat like some rescindable grace. To only two other souls in all the earth had she spoken of them aloud: to Clem, with whom she'd wished silently, breathlessly, like a young girl over a cakeful of pink candles, that this unlikely gift might arrive intact at their doorsteps; and to the man in the D-backs gift shop, where she had confessed giddily, repeatedly, with each irresistible purchase that she was just getting a few things "for my grandson." There were moments she was convinced it was as simple as that—

"I was just wondering," Gabby continued, "If they've picked them up by any chance."

The ticket woman sucked a remnant from between her teeth and said tartly, "Well, did they show up in the seats?"

The foolishness of her inquiry had not, until that moment, been fully evident. "Well, no," Gabby said sheepishly. "I'm not even sure they're coming, really. I just thought, you know, I'd check."

"What's the name?"

Like breath held in a tunnel, Gabby released the words. "Oberdorf. Jill and Gus Oberdorf."

She watched as the woman thumbed disinterestedly through the box of small envelopes. "Nope, still here. You want me to sell 'em?"

Gabby's hand flew up like a deflector shield. "No. I'd like to leave them here. Just in case."

Maybe she should have been more assertive in her letter, extended the sort of invitation one marks on a calendar. Gabby tried to recall if, in their one brief meeting, Jill had seemed the forgiving type. In truth, she remembered very little about her except that the waiter had inquired if they were mother and daughter. It was possible, Gabby conceded, that she had winced in response. Battling anew the demons of eviscerating doubt—of what might have been, might be, might never be, not ever—Gabby stopped at a beer cart en route to her seat, and in way that sounded suddenly pitiful, said, "One, please."

The fat lady redux.

At the end of the ninth inning, the game was tied at eight runs apiece, a feat that had taken six Diamondback pitchers, including the Closer, to accomplish. Clem and the bullpen catcher were the only men still standing. "What'd I tell you?" Gus said. "They were just saving him. "

Had they called Clem in in the fifth or the sixth or the seventh, Jill would have cheered as loudly as anyone, but now the stakes were just too high. Gus laid his hand on his mother's knee and said, "Here we go."

Top of the tenth. All eyes—43,331 times two—were on the bullpen gate.

Binoculars were not needed to see that it remained shut.

Instead, from the Arizona dugout, the closing pitcher stepped up and out and, hopping over the third baseline for luck, reclaimed the mound.

"What're they doing?!! " Gus shouted. "He's already thrown 23 pitches. This guy's never good for more than 25."

Jill knew she was supposed to share Gus's indignation, to want nothing more than for Clem to take the mound in front of his son and be the hero of the game. But who could promise an ending like that? As long as Clem stayed where he was, he could do no wrong.

"I'm sure the coach knows what he's doing."

The Closer walked the first batter.

"See, what'd I tell you!" Gus threw his arms in the air. "Maybe now they'll wise up."

Still, the next batter stepped into the box and the extra-inning game continued.

"Crap!"

Jill raised a disapproving brow.

Gus buried his face in his binoculars and watched as the 10-million-dollar Closer threw four straight balls to load a second base runner. This was no longer personal: this was baseball. Rising up, a lone voice in the cheap seats, Gus shouted, "Bring in McGaffey!"

He did not cease. He did not sit.

Moved by the kid's enthusiasm and the opportunity to shout, the beer-soused frat house behind him joined in, U of A students too young to know that Clem McGaffey was once one of the finest pitchers the state had ever produced.

"Bring in McGaffey!" they bellowed, and the plea began to swell.

Jumping to her feet, Jill too began to chant. "Bring in McGaffey! Bring in McGaffey!"

The third batter was hit in the thigh with a misplaced curve ball and the bleachers went wild. "Bring in McGaffey! Bring in McGaffey!!

In the bullpen, Clem bore down on his warm-up pitches, which seemed to grow harder and faster as the chanting grew louder. Like Mike Mulligan and his Steam Shovel working harder and faster to the delight of the crowd, Jill thought. Like that children's book she used to read to Clem when he was little— the one with the steam shovel, Gabby mused; what was it called?

On the screen, the spontaneous uprising in the bleachers was projected. Gus and Jill were obscured by the hundred standing fans surrounding them as Gabby rose to her feet and threw her wary voice in with the crowd—"Bring in McGaffey!"—until soon it was not just the spirited youth of the High Pavilion but the low seats and the front seats and even the starchy, golf-shirted executive crowd behind the backstop— all of them on their feet, on their seats, stomping and clapping and shouting for no reason beyond the incomparable sound of newfound hope. "Bring in McGaffey!!!"

Mulishly, the manager resisted, standing arms folded as the waning Closer tossed ball one, ball two, ball three; finally, as if it had been his grand strategy all along, he stepped out onto the field to remove him.

And so it was, with the bases loaded, that Clem McGaffey bowed his head at the bullpen gate and blazed out across left field, the outcome of the Arizona defense wholly resting on his long-ignored shoulders.

Ordinarily an unknown pitcher in a moment such as this was greeted with tittering silence, but momentum had already paved the way for Clem's arrival. The crowd was committed.

The dye was cast. Madness erupting in waves and whoops and bouncing beach balls, the fans cried out for their underdog hero.

"Bring it on, McGaffey! Bring it on, McGaffey!" they shouted, thumbing through the nacho-gummed programs at their feet for his bio.

Clem threw two warm-up pitches and the ump cued the fourth batter who was standing in wait with a 3-0 count. Gus held his breath, his mother's sleeve, as with three straight pitches—a curve, and a knuckleball, and a change-up, Gus reported—Clem got the first out of the inning.

"That's my dad," he said to the frat boys who were howling too loudly to hear him.

Lifting her binoculars, Jill reached out across the field to share from afar the maternal thrill, to bridge the gap. In a sea of raucous strangers Gabby looked like an abandoned bird. Jill considered the empty seats beside her and how they might get to them, but there was no time. The winning run was on third.

From the stretch, Clem stared him down.

The base runner danced and teased and quickly flopped to his belly as Clem forced him back with a stealth bullet. The base runner rose and, like a hermit crab crossing the road, once again began to inch his way down along the final 90-foot stretch. Clem ignored him, throwing a fastball so high and sweet the new batter could not resist, popping out on the first swing.

Two down.

The din in the sealed, metallic dome was like a rock concert in a submarine. Jill threw her arms around Gus and together they screamed and bumped and jumped up and down until the cleanup hitter stepped into the box, silencing them both, silencing them all. When Clem's first pitch whistled just past his knees, the sonic floodgates burst.

"We love McGaffey! We love McGaffey!"

Pitch number two came and went, and with it, the yelp of "Strike Two!"

From the bottom of her unanchored soul Jill pleaded *please God* and, in a single remarkable moment, the burden of unknowing inexplicably lifted: pain gone, worry gone, and in their stead, spilling over like champagne cocktail from a wedding fountain, was the wonder of the beneficent choreography that had led them to be here for this.

Had the roof not been sealed, Jill would have heard the storm outside. Felt the rumble of the thunder. Seen the heralding lightning clap.

"WE LOVE MCGAFFEY! WE LOVE MCGAFFEY!!

Heaven and Hell was the realm of the 0-and-2 pitch. Gabby'd been around long enough to know that. Clem lifted his leg and she cupped her hands to her face like a ventilator. Without this last out, nothing her son had done up until this moment would count for a thing. Pinching her eyes shut, she tried to envision what destiny, in a good and just world, would look like. It seemed like such a small request, this one, tiny little out. But with quantum rebellion, the earth failed to comply. The crack of the bat was so distinctive Gabby didn't even have to look. No one did. Even the outfielders dug in their heels and gaped as the ball soared like a passing jet overhead. On a reflex, Gus lifted his glove, but there was no risk in him catching it; that grand slam ball went clear beyond the highest seat and into the geodesic beams, ricocheting off the panels, working its way down through the metal side walls as if through a gauntlet of high fives, before landing in a back dumpster with a grave thud.

Baseball was a merciless game. Even before the fourth base runner crossed the plate, many of the fickle crowd had begun to shuffle out. Few who remained had it in them to cheer for a rally; they had put their faith in Clem McGaffey (who?) and Clem McGaffey had failed them. Kicking off at the bottom of the order, the D-backs went down in three and proved what Gabby had known all along: God was cruel. The only small gratitude she could muster was the fact that the boy had not been here to see it.

An opening.

In the wake of Clem's failure a new chorus of sounds emerged: the squawk of dustpans, roll top doors, the echo of scattering, caterwauling fans. From the third floor men's room came the sound of retching, and fast on its heels, the grinding cataclysm of gears. Jill looked up. The sky itself seemed to be parting as BOB's clever roof slowly opened to an awning of pure, sun-dazzled blue. Swiftly the sequestered disappointment of thousands was spirited away in the warm desert air.

"Why don't we do this..." Jill began. "Why don't we go back to the hotel and take a swim..."

"I'm not leaving until I see him."

Jill wasn't entirely sure that his plan didn't include holding vigil in these seats until the next day's game. And the next. "Gus..."

"I want to see my dad."

"Honey," she said and reached for his hand. "I'm not sure he's going to be up to meeting anyone right now."

Gus pulled his hand free and stood up so fast and straight Jill realized it would be a matter of months, not years, before he passed her. "I'm not anyone," he said, and kicking over his souvenir cup of Coke, headed for the exit.

In the eye of the beholder.

The other Diamondback players had already come and gone. Gus counted them off by name, by number, by position, by batting average. Like a cop on a stakeout, he leaned on the dash of their rented sedan and scanned the perimeter with his binoculars. It was nearly six o'clock before Gabby and Clem, who held his head as if the sun, even at this late hour, was just too bright, emerged through the back door. Jill turned off the ignition. The engine cracked and soughed and settled in the heat, as an eerie silence quickly supplanted the pleasantly distracting, air-conditioned whirr.

"Do you want me to go first?" she asked.

"No. I'll go." Gus's hand was already on the door. There was no hesitation, no holding back. Stepping out of the car he shouted across the blocked-off street, "Dad!"

Clem and Gabby kept on walking, following the curve of the building around, away. Jill stepped out of the car ready for— what, she couldn't say. Gus started to run, his clunky, unlaced sneakers thumping on the hot asphalt as he called out again, louder still, "Da-ad!! "

Clem and Gabby were no more than six feet away, close enough for them to hear his footsteps, his breath.

Gus tried again. "Mr. McGaffey," he said, and at this Clem turned.

Jill reached for the binoculars, tried to read his lips.

"Sorry, son," Clem said, patting down his pockets, "I don't have a pen."

Gus straightened his spine, rolled back his shoulders, planted his two gangly legs in the hard ground. "I don't want your autograph."

"Well," Clem said, "I can't blame you there."

Gabby stared at Gus like a photo from her own mantle. "Clem," she whispered, afraid a raised voice might make him disappear, "It's him."

Gus confirmed it with a proud nod. "It's me."

The chasm between them groaned like an iceberg. Clem looked to his mother, his shoes, the boy, the woman across the lot who appeared to be inching towards them. Gabby opened her mouth to help them along but the void was already filled. Throwing his arms around his father's neck like the best welcome home in the world, Gus exclaimed, "You were great, Dad."

Clem had no choice but to smile. "You must have slipped out before the end."

Gus swatted Clem's arm. "So you gave up one dinger, so what. It's not like you loaded the bases, or anything. Not like me. Like two days ago when I was pitching in Sectionals— that's like this really huge all-star tournament—"

"I remember Sectionals," Clem said. Gabby saw her son's eyes brighten like a window with the screens removed.

220

"You do? Did you win 'em?"

"Nope."

"Us neither. I'm telling you, you should have seen these guys we had to play. They were monsters. I couldn't get anything past them. Bottom of the first inning, right..." Gus raised his palms in a gesture so familiar, Gabby had to bite down on her lip to keep from laughing. "First I loaded the bases, then I walked in two runs. Then I gave up a Grand Slam. You want to talk about bad. Now that's bad." Turning abruptly to Gabby, he held out his hand. "I'm Gus, by the way."

"Gabriella," she said as they shook, "But you may call me Gabby if you like."

"I think I'd rather call you grandma, if that's okay."

Now it was Clem's turn to bury his tickled lip. "Yeah, grandma, how 'bout it?"

Gabby folded her arms across her chest and said, "Why don't we discuss it with your mother."

A trio of heads turned back in search of Jill who stood now two Clem-lengths away. She took three baby steps forward. Clem did the same, no more, no less. Face to face, the air was left clear for objections, recriminations. What transpired between them offered no clues as obvious as these, but rather a sort of psychic, optic morass of assessing, pleading, second guessing; of searching for a mending thread in the silence of their reciprocated gaze. Clem placed his hands on Jill's shoulders and, in a voice that reserved judgment, said,

"Thanks for coming."

Like a spaniel puppy, Gus reappeared at Clem's side and reclaimed the moment. "So, dad," he said, "Do you think you could teach me your knuckleball? I'm telling you, Hoyt Wilhelm's got nothing on you."

The sun beamed down though the parting desert clouds and Clem smiled, pleased. "Fan of ol' Wilhelm's, huh?"

"He's a fan of everything about everything about baseball," Jill said.

"Guess it's in the genes, right dad?"

The foursome gravitated into a neat and sturdy square from which Gabby spoke out in Jill's defense. "I imagine your mother has had a thing or two to do with your baseball education."

"Are you kidding?" Gus cleaved to his father. "Do you know what she calls the bullpen?"

"Now, Gus—" Jill said with no particular firmness. She had prepared herself for a far stiffer penance than this.

"The pitcher's lounge," Gus said, flashing his mom a playful grin. "Can you believe that? It's a miracle I've made it this far."

"You wanna see it?" Clem offered.

"What?"

"The pitcher's lounge," he said, and winked at Jill in a way that bound them, if nothing else, as parents.

Jill blushed as her son, their son, leapt three feet off the

222

ground. "Sure."

"C'mon," he said, and began to lead them back into the stadium which only moments before Gabby feared he might never again enter with his head held high.

"Why don't you boys go," Gabby suggested. She patted Jill's arm with a gracious squeeze. "We'll wait right here."

The touch of Gabby's hand took Jill by surprise. It was like a long-forgotten back rub, like her mother stroking her angel's wings under the ruffle of her favorite Lanz nightie.

Tipping into Gabby's arms, Jill broke. "I'm sorry."

Her needy body fell against a space so long abandoned Gabby had almost forgotten it existed. "Ssssh, it's all right, it's okay." Gabby swaddled Jill in her arms, stroked her hair, cooed, even. "Everything's going to be all right."

Like a chick, Jill peeped, "Are you sure?"

Gabby wiped Jill's eyes and lifted her chin and with matriarchal certainty declared, "I have a really good feeling about this."

The long goodbye.

They had tried to go their separate ways after dinner. Then after a trip to the arcade. Then after drinks in the lobby of the Holiday Inn where Gabby insisted they should no longer be staying; the next day, after the game—a game in which Gus sat in the family section close enough to the dugout to scrutinize the manager's notes on the lineup card (Clem's name was nowhere to be found) and Gabby and Jill got drunk on draft beer, pinking the cheeks of their parallel lives—they moved out to the spare room in Cortaro, their departure plans, left vague.

And so it went, the days, the nights, as tacitly they conspired, Gabby and Gus and Jill and Clem, to shuffle their feet on the stoop in the moonlight postponing their uncharted goodbyes.

Naturally, they'd have to stay for Gus's birthday. And the hot air balloon races. And there was still another homestand before the team went on the road...

And then... And then...

All good things.

Six days had passed like a blink, like a lifetime, every moment a surreal and spinning dream. It wasn't until after the final game of the second homestand, when Clem had been unceremoniously tapped on the shoulder by a lackey from the head office, that time seemed to slow. Interminable was the wait outside the Bank One gates. Gabby paced. Gus tossed a tennis ball against the brick façade, fielding the hops off the gummy promenade. Jill, left alone with her own thoughts just long enough to remember the summer school students she'd dumped with a sub and a claim of strep throat, checked her messages. Only one was noteworthy: the head of the English department informing her in less-than-poetic language that if she missed another day there would not be a job waiting for her in the fall. "I am, as we speak," the message warned, "staring at a stack of good applicants." These were the words that underscored the moment when Clem finally reappeared carrying not one, but four duffel bags. Even before he set them on the ground, he looked, somehow, lighter.

"Well?" Gabby said.

"Well, I guess that's that."

Gabby searched her son's eyes, his brow, the muscles along his perfect jaw line for signs of despair. She found instead an unlikely softness, as if all the signs of struggle and doubt had been air-brushed right out of him. His eyes, which had for as far back as she could remember been fixed in a sort of defensive, sun-blind squint, were now open and easy; a man at peace: a man who'd at long last been told the truth about where he stood and was, by that knowledge, set free.

The news was not as salvific for Gus. Screwing his face up like a nasty sinker he shouted, "Whatdaya mean that's that?"

"Gus—" Jill began, but Clem stepped in, stepped down.

Kneeling before his son, he met his eye. "I mean, it looks like baseball's down to one McGaffey, buddy."

A glimpse of the boy Clem and Gabby had missed out on made a surprise appearance: Gus at three, his lips pursed and quavering, his brown eyes pinched and bugging to accommodate tears he refused to shed. Shouting a word the women pretended not to hear, he hurled, with all the outraged heft he could muster, the tennis ball at the sign on the door that read *Management*.

"Alright Gus, let's not burn any bridges," Clem said.

"And what does that mean?"

Clem and Jill exchanged resonant glances that stopped just short; always just short.

Draping his arm around Gus's shoulder Clem said, "We'll talk about it over dinner."

And so it was, over platters of ribs and beans and slaw that the newly-bound foursome raised their glasses and refused to look back.

"To the future!" Clem proclaimed.

"To the future," Gabby chimed, their mugs meeting in the center with a hearty clank. Theirs was a toast of vague good cheer about the wholly uncertain, but to Gus it must have seemed like something else entirely. Lifting his root beer soberly, reverently, like an acolyte at a Christmas mass, he fixed his small, perfect jaw and nodded. "To the future."

Jill knew all too well those resolute eyes. Felt the weight of them in her own dreaming heart. She wanted to rescue him, to tell Gus that he'd misunderstood— that the future didn't literally mean him—but realized, as she opened her mouth to speak, that what was intended, what was inferred, was no longer hers to determine. Somewhere between Gus's first pair of cleats and now, she had lost the power to control how he perceived the world.

As losses go, it was less painful than most. Nothing could have prevented it— not a father, not grandparents. Time, was all it was. Gus was 12 now. Old enough to start drawing his own conclusions. Old enough to begin, with pieces of visions both guided and mis, to spin his own web. Whether standing on the shoulders of his father's broken dream was inherently good or bad, right or wrong, whether it would catapult him into the stratosphere or topple them both, Jill could not say; and what would be the point if she did?

With an acquiescent sigh, she lifted her glass and, just as she had a dozen years before, willed herself to smile. "To the future."

So many fields.

This was why kids couldn't be trusted to make their own decisions: they couldn't see the big picture. They couldn't comprehend the scope of the human landscape of America. As the early morning flight lifted up over the pinking Arizona sky, the first field appeared through Jill's window. She smiled, pressed her hand to the glass like a fool, as if the fact of a baseball field could only be some cosmic farewell meant for her and her alone. It was only a matter of time—four minutes, to be exact—before, gazing down through the scratched Plexiglas frame, she saw, through the parting clouds, the second field. Another good sign, a happy sign. Redundant, perhaps, but nonetheless it made Jill think fondly about the boys and how they would likely be spending the next two weeks: playing catch and fungo and MLB video games on the ridiculously expensive system Clem'd bought for Gus's birthday. Gus probably wouldn't brush his teeth for a week.

"Good morning, ladies and gentleman, this is your captain speaking," the pilot said. "If you look just up ahead on our left, you'll see the baseball fields of our own West Phoenix Little League team. Last night, these twelve talented local boys won the Regional Championships and are now on their way to the Little League World Series in Williamsport, Pennsylvania. We wish 'em all the best of luck!"

Many on the plane burst out in spontaneous applause. Jill squinted down at the cluster of fields, numbers three, four and five on her count, in search of telltale greatness, perfidy.

"Bloody Mary?" the flight attendant purred.

"Um…" Jill said.

Fueled by vodka and the swiftly passing miles, the burr at the core of her psyche grew to the size of eighteen fields. Eighteen fields in the first half of a single, unextraordinary short hop. Eighteen fields before they'd even come close to the outer limits, let alone the dense grid, of the baseball-loving, superstar-breeding Southland. Eighteen fields times how many flight paths? How many towns? How many all-stars in new satin jackets? She could see them now, lined up end to quantum end, across the mountains and the deserts and the prairies and the seas, from one coast to the other and back again, and still, no doubt, there'd be go-to pitchers to spare.

Jill slammed the vinyl window shade shut. Her head began to swim lightly in the tomatoey haze. Hows and whys floated, swarmed. Every bird in God's aviary had landed on Clem McGaffey's shoulder, and for what? Where had it gotten him? Left him? Left them all? And would he say that it was worth it? Would she? Would Gus? What measure of greatness had been planted in their son and would it be sufficient to the dream? Or would she and Clem, a dozen years from now— (Jill paused to picture it)— be picking up the pieces of their son's imperfect quest at some godforsaken farm league bus stop? And who was to say he'd even make it that far?

Jill slid the window shade back open just a crack and, like a teenager peeking through split fingers at a horror flick, forced herself to look—nineteen, twenty—through the eyes of hindsight at the glaring, exponential truth. Never had the theory of Meant-to-Be seemed more like pie in the sky.

Alone at last.

Jill had waited a dozen years for this. Time alone without distractions. Time alone without obligations. Whole nights full of empty hours with which to mine the riches of her heart in artful prose. She'd start tomorrow. Just as soon as she'd unpacked and ran a load of laundry and called Gus and checked in at school and picked up some groceries, and well, she did vow to clean the carpets before the summer, but after that, it was just going to be writing, writing, writing— no interruptions, no derailed thoughts. Just her and the blank page. Just like back at U of A. Only different, better. By the time Gus got home, she'd be well underway. Surely, momentum would carry her through the fall and all its demands. By Christmas she might even have a first draft, she smiled, and as if the thought were a *fait accompli*, popped a video in the VCR to celebrate.

By day three, her after school schedule was diversion-free. All she had to do was pick up some new boxers for Gus and then it was straight home to her desk. Twenty minutes, in and out, tops, an estimate that was not so much inaccurate as naive. Jill had not factored in the location of the junior boy's department, directly across from cosmetics. She had not planned on the woman with the honeyed voice and the lashes thick and shiny as mink offering to show her a few tips. She had not fully recognized the depth of own pulchritudinous neglect.

"Why don't we start with a little toner," the woman said. Her name tag read in cursive red letters: Chloey. Settling Jill onto a tall, pink stool—comfy?—she doused a cotton ball with something cool and crisp and strangely reminiscent of the sachets Jill's mother used to keep in her nightgown drawer. Chloey swiped the ball of cool, cotton across Jill's face, which tingled with a peppermint chill. Such a small and wonderful thing, to be touched, to be served; two minutes in the chair and Jill felt as if she'd died and gone to a day spa.

"You really do have lovely skin."

Jill opened her eyes and said in a half-whisper, "Thank you."

Under Chloey's powdery spell Jill yielded, awakened anew to the reality that she inhabited a body and that people could see it. She was embarrassed, now, in this setting, to admit she wore no base. That she'd been using the same moisturizer, the same lip gloss, the same drugstore brand of mascara since grad school; her kohl liner had simply dried up over time and never been replaced.

"And what's this one for?" Jill inquired with delight, fingering the glistening jars and tubes like a child in Willie Wonka's. Had she ever seriously considered dating, she might have given more thought to her appearance, but there had been no time for anything as extraneous as men. Besides, dating was about searching and searching was about void, and Jill had never felt that either of those conditions applied to her. And so each morning she'd washed her face and brushed her teeth and pulled her hair back in a sensible knot and, funneling all her self-improving urges into her son, waited for her time to come again. She could see it clear as lake water, just like the book she had yet to conceive.

"There!" Chloey said proudly, spinning Jill around toward the mirror. "Beautiful."

A ripple rose up from her lap to lips, which parted with pleasure to agree.

Of course, all the nuances of her new and improved face would be lost in a frame of unfinished hair; that's what Chloey had said when she handed Jill the card for a stylist that charged ten times what she was used to paying at Supercuts. Under a spigot of suds, he rubbed her neck and offered her sherry. Like a sculptor to clay, he eyed her jaw, her cheeks, her ears. He basted her loveless tresses in cremes and elixirs and folded them in plumes of foil. Even before she'd handed over the tip, Jill swore she'd never do it again. But as the store windows teased her with glimpses of carefree layers dancing vibrantly in the sun, her only regret was that she hadn't done it sooner. Before their trip to Arizona, say.

Naturally, her new look did not go unnoticed on campus. When one of her coworkers suggested a drink, Jill was unable to come up with a single reason to decline. Over chopped salads and white wine she practiced the art of adult conversation, dabbled in double entendre for no other reason than to see if she remembered how. The man was an associate professor of comparative religion, a man who knew everything and believed nothing. He reached for Jill's hand over tiramisu. She withdrew it so quickly she wiped out the cappuccino. "I'm sorry," she said with a shrug, blotting, rising. "But I've got a pile of exams this high."

And so the days passed. And so the blank pages remained. The problem, Jill told herself, was not so much that she lacked discipline, but that writing was not the only need that had gone so long ignored.

In my house there are many boxes.

The appearance of a grandchild had made Gabby nostalgic. In the one-car garage, which, like everything else in the newly-minted exburbs of Arizona, was clean and beige and cobweb free, she ran her eye along a tall, shelved stack of shipping boxes. The movers had unloaded them straight from the truck two years back and, other than the ones marked *Christmas Ornaments, Christmas Linens, Christmas Lights,* they had remained untouched, on hold, posterity waiting for a recipient. Everything was neatly labeled. *Baby clothes, Ski clothes, Toys, Books, Games.* Gabby stepped up on a stool to remove the one marked *Little League*. She was surprised, as she pulled it down, to see another box behind it. She slid it up to the lip of the shelf and turned it around once, twice. On the back side it read, in a fat, slapdash scrawl of blue Sharpie, **U of A stuff**. Gabby eyed the box as if it were ticking. Clem must had dropped it off back in Atlanta sometime, maybe on his way to Vero Beach. It must have been moved into storage with all the rest, and finally back here, where it sat, now awaiting her deliberation.

If only she knew what had really gone on between Jill and Clem, the breadth and the depth of it. If only she had some framework by which to judge all the ineffable glances they'd exchanged throughout the visit. Gabby had come to

236

understand, over the course of their time together, that Jill had once loved Clem enough to let him go, to chase his dream, but she could not say with any certainty how her own son felt. Not then, not now. If there was someone he confided in in these matters, it was not her.

Gabby reached for the scissors, fanned them open like a scythe. Freed from the slit tape, the contents burst forth, first, a wadded up, blue and red U of A windshirt, still soiled with the sweat of his last appearance in the College World Series. Gabby set it aside, made a mental note to wash it, dug deeper. There was a program from each of Clem's seasons there, his biography growing in length and stature with each year. There was a wrist-grip and a gyro-ball and a therapeutic rubber cord for warm-ups. There was a napkin from a restaurant named Pancho's, and a packet of Swiss Miss cocoa. There were a dozen baseball caps and, at the very bottom of the box, wrapped in one of the monogrammed washcloths Gabby had given him to take to college, a single book of poetry: *The Collected Sonnets of John Donne*.

Gabby opened it slowly to find the inscription.

To my beloved #17,
May my voice soothe you to sleep forever.
Jill

Gabby laid her hands on the type as if to muzzle the

words. How could so few of them change so much? Why had she been so quick to assume that a girl could never have meant as much to Clem as the game? The four tight walls of the garage began to press in. Her own husband's considerable shelves had been lined with a thousand volumes of poetry, but not once in their twenty-seven years of marriage had he read her a single verse aloud. Certainly there was a fondness there, but in her heart she knew she would have traded it all for the role of Giselle and a shower of admiring roses. She had no firsthand knowledge of the kind of love that trumps everything, was not—in her defense—predisposed to suspect it.

From the center of the book, the yellowed edge of an envelope peeked out. It was addressed to Jill, in Los Angeles, and stamped with an official postal mark: RETURN TO SENDER, ADDRESS UNKNOWN. Gabby was not prepared to read the letter. She might have held it in her hands for a minute or an hour or the whole accusing day.

Dear Jilly-

Where are you??? I've called a thousand times, left a thousand messages. Tonight I got some recording and, idiot that I am, I want to believe it's cause you can't live without me. I'm looking at the door right now, like it's really going to open and you're really going to walk back in it and read me to sleep. I can't sleep, Jilly. I can't think. The only time I can focus is when I'm on the mound.

Did I do something to make you mad? Tell me, please! If you found someone else I'll understand. I know you deserve better, like some fancy professor with a million degrees or something, and I even think I could be happy for you, eventually. But not like this. Not if we can't even speak or be friends or anything.

Last week we had our opening game against USC. (Maybe you read about it in the paper, I hope you did.) The whole time I was on the bus, driving from the airport to the field, I just kept wondering if one of those apartments was yours, and if you were home. I was even thinking maybe you'd show up at the game and surprise me. I kept looking up in the stands at the place where you always like to sit, just along the first baseline, but there were just a bunch of rich frat boys and parents and cheerleader types. Boring, stupid. If I use the word "vapid," will you change your mind?

I wish so badly you were here right now. The daytime's not so bad, but at night I feel like I can't stand to be in this stupid dorm without you. If you knocked on my door right now and said let's go, I think I might just do it. Just run away. Maybe we could go to Ohio. I'd like to see where you grew up. I'd like to see that gardening shed in your backyard where you used to write in your journal and drink hot chocolate. I'd like to stand beside you at the lake and hold you while you cry. So let's go there okay? Let's just drive all night and you can tell me whatever it is I did wrong and I'll fix it, I promise and then we could stop in some crappy motel and make love. I miss your beautiful body like crazy. I know that's not very poetic, but it's true, babe. So just call me, okay. Call me so I can hear your voice. I just need to hear your voice.

I love you,

C

Last chance.

On the eve of Gus's return, Jill made her peace with what she'd failed to accomplish and, zapping a bowl of Kettlecorn, sat down to watch the Dodger game. The bases were loaded and Shawn Green was on deck. Jill found herself studying the way he tapped his bat against the arch of his cleat, the lazy, pendulum swing of it, the way he stood in his body like a picnicker in the Jell-O line. His eyes, though, told a different story. Everything he could do with that bat was in those eyes. Jill leaned forward and reached for a pen, and just like that, the TV went black. As if the life source had been sucked clear out of the city with a straw, the whole apartment fell dark and throbbed with a velvet quiet.

In the pitch, Jill grew strangely hopeful. Obstacles were good. Obstacles, Jill told her students each day, created conflict. Obstacles forced characters to rise to greater heights. Groping her way to the kitchen she passed up a flashlight in favor of matches, and like Laura Ingalls Wilder, carried a single brass candlestick to the bedroom. She set it on the family desk beside the pen and the ink and the watermarked paper which had long lain gathering dust. The flicker of light cast a golden ellipse across the knotty wood, framing her face like a cameo pin. Reaching for the quill and the words she had waited the better part of a lifetime for, Jill dipped it in the ink pot and pressed down.

The boy stepped out on the soft, green grass, the dewy, sun-kissed grass, the fresh, green-smelling—

No, scratch that. Jill balled up the page and withdrew a new sheet and, tilting the nib into the deep and patient ink, began again.

The boy stepped out onto the great green field as if onto a magic carpet...

Then you'll be a man, my son.

That's not what dad says. That's not the way dad does it. Two weeks alone with his father and suddenly nothing Jill said or did was right, or even, apparently, relevant. Me and dad—

"Dad and I," she corrected.

"Me and dad," Gus repeated, digging in his cleats, "Watched games every night."

"That was summer. This is school time."

"So?"

"So, you have homework. I happen to know for a fact that you have a book report due Friday on *To Kill a Mockingbird*."

"Who told you that?"

"I ran into Meg Reimers and her mother at the market." Gus upped the volume with an impertinent thumb. Jill planted herself like a bouncer in front of the TV, arms folded, elbows wide, and pressed him. "So?"

"So, what?" Gus craned around his obstruction of a mother till she could see the ropey muscles along the side of his neck.

It was only a matter of time (years? days?) before Gus would be able to bodily remove her from his view. With teetering power, Jill persisted, "So, have you even started it yet?"

"I've got it under control, mom. Just move, wouldja."

"What do you mean you've got it under control? I haven't seen you read a single page at home, so unless you—"

"AUUAGHH!" Gus let out an exasperated moan as if Jill's very being was unbearable to him. "Mom. Get a life! No one but you and a few other geeks actually read books anymore."

How long had she fought the urge to just give up, give in, to join the ranks of all the other worn-down parents who'd finally just rolled over. "Well, perhaps you'd like to enlighten me then, on how you and all these bold new illiterates plan to write the book report?"

"Just download the cheats."

Jill cocked her head. "The cheats?"

"Yeah, mom, the cheats. It tells you, like all the main people and stuff they do and, you know, all the main—" Gus formed his hand in sarcastic air-quotes and said, "Conflicts, and things."

"Cliff Notes, in other words."

"Whatever."

His rudeness she would deal with later, but the forgoing of *To Kill A Mockingbird*, this Jill could not stand idly by for. With a sweeping and incontrovertible tug, she yanked the cord from the wall. Gus's eyes, the screen, caved in on themselves with the same shrinking gasp.

"What are you doing? I'm watching the game!!"

"You can read the box scores in the morning. They'll tell you everything you need to know. All the main people and the stuff they do and the—" Jill aped his mocking quote fingers, "Main conflicts and things."

Gus stormed with such bluster Jill feared she might be knocked to the ground by wind sheer alone. "I hate it here. I mean it. I want to go live with dad!!"

Jill followed him to the door, which was promptly slammed. She addressed the wood. "You don't think your dad will make you do homework? Your dad went to a good college, mister. A college where he read a lot of books and wrote a lot of good reports on them." She left out the part about having a lot of good help.

"Pro ball players don't have to write book reports!"

"Fine," she shouted. "The day you're drafted, you don't ever have to pick up a book again. Until then, get started."

Jill crouched down in the hallway, trembling and spent. Anyone would have known that a boy so long deprived of a father would now want nothing but. Jill knew it. She was well aware that they were now entering a predictable chapter of conflict from which they would not emerge unchanged. But the form and the scope and the tenor of these changes, these were beyond her. These were strictly the writer's domain. Pressing her brow bones against her bent knees, Jill tried to envision what the author of her life story already knew: where they were in the greater narrative and which were the red herrings and whether the crisis would be prolonged and how many times they'd get it wrong before the bitter seeds of this moment, of her thirty-seven years, would flower unimaginably into something perfectly wonderful.

On the ceiling above, the glow-in-the-dark stars that had once acted as a nightlight from Gus's room to mommy had grown dim. Jill lifted her hands in the dark, groping, as if the schematic of her days was already printed in the charged atoms and could be trusted to adhere to the rules of literature. What choice did she have? The author of her life wouldn't be pressing an ear under the crack of her son's room for the sound of turned pages. The author of her life wouldn't be worried about a thing. The hallway filled, suddenly, or so it seemed to Jill, with the unmistakable scent of peat moss and damp terra cotta and all the rusty trowels that had filled the shed where she had once cocooned, pen in hand, envisioning the future when every good thing still lay ahead. Jill closed her eyes, tilted her face towards the stars (were they shining, now, just a little?) and, breathing deep the sentient reassurance, trusted with a child's heart that the author of her life kept his promises.

Spurt.

No adolescent boy in the history of progeny had ever grown like this before. Daily, hourly, like some ridiculous sunflower, Gus shot right up out of his own body, his bright, incredulous face bobbing atop his new stem. Jill braced herself against the counter as he rounded the corner each morning for breakfast. She met his gaze, she met his chin, she met the shoulders that seemed to be thickening like bread dough left to rise in the sun. He went through shoes like Dixie cups. Pants failed to close at the waist or reach down to the ankle mere days after purchase. Her incredulity led to a series of markings on the wall which she backed him up against at such an alarming frequency, and with such regular incremental results, that on the rare days when he hadn't, in fact, grown taller overnight, she felt disappointed. Inch by inch by testosterone-laced inch Gus grew. Five-one, five-two, five-three. He seemed to skip right over four and go straight to five. By the time he'd begun his first season in the North Palms 13/14 year old division, Gus was 5'6". His arms no longer hung like spindles at his side, but seemed to rise up on themselves like beach pails on a shoulder iron. Five-seven, five-eight. He left home to circle the bases. By the time he came in, Jill was reaching for the ruler, backing him up against the wall, turning her head away shyly from his developing chest. Five-nine. Five-ten.

Clem called almost nightly now. With the phone in one hand and a barbell in the other, Gus gazed in the mirror, assessing his evolving form.

"Gus, honey, could you help me with the water bottle?"

"One second, mom." It was not a stall, but an estimate. Dutifully bidding his father goodnight, Gus retrieved the ten-gallon bottle from the bottom of the stairs and flipped it like a juggler's club into its cooler. "Anything else?" His voice was as deep as a doting newlywed's.

"No, that's it. Thanks," Jill said to his chin and resisted the urge to remeasure.

Détente had come in inches and days. As if the act of growing had somehow exorcised the demons from his contentious bones, her son was, once again, free and easy in his own skin. His bimonthly visits to Tucson, where Clem had taken a job as the pitching coach at their alma mater, no doubt helped, too.

The baseball season was strangely pleasant. Rod Dempster had left North Palms in search of greener pastures. Gus's coach, who knew only slightly more about the game than Jill, respected the pitch count limits and rest days that Clem had requested. Fewer parents came to watch and those who did seemed unconcerned with the score. For a year or two, likely their last, they were content simply to watch the progression of their sons' virility: the stunning new distances of their throws, the loose and bawdy camaraderie in the dugout, the way the girls caught the boys' eyes in the golden light of spring evenings, stirring sweet aches in their own aging limbs. For one brief season, they were all granted a reprieve, from goals or futures or any greater purpose than strong, young bodies rejoicing beneath the fading periwinkle sky.

"He can't go another year without good coaching, Jill." This, over the phone, as the season, the school year came to an end. "If he really wants to play this game I need him here with me."

Blood converged on the drum of Jill's ear as if to the source of a wound. It was not shocking, the news, the suggestion. She had waited all year for him to say it. But preparation is all in the mind; the body never feels it coming.

"I know," Jill said, just that. No more.

Gus was the easy part. He needed to be with Clem and Clem needed to be there—it was just that simple—but where did that leave her? It was a free country, of course. Clem couldn't stop her from entering the state, finding a job, a little two-bedroom apartment where Gus could come visit on alternate Thursdays.

"Would you really hate it? Moving back here, again?" The roiling blood in Jill's ears paused, parted. Clem must have heard it through the phone. "I mean, it would make things easier. For Gus."

"For Gus," she refrained. "Right. Absolutely."

"I could check the job board, see if there's any openings

in the English department."

"There are." The truth leapt out before she could stop it. "I mean, I think there might be. I was just sort of messing around, online. You know, for Gus."

"So good, then," Clem said as if something like progress had been made. "So, you know, maybe we'll see."

"Yeah," Jill said, curling her toes in the shape of a smile. "Maybe we'll see."

The lost boys.

They gathered on the curb in front of the 7-11, banging, crashing, grinding, seething, daring each other to break the wrists they once used to turn double plays. With their ripped shirts and their flat, soulless eyes, Jill hardly recognized them anymore. One of the boys—was his name Mickey?—used to cry, she remembered, every time he struck out. She didn't recall ever seeing a mom; only a dad— a large, gruff, taciturn man who spent most of his son's limited playing time tailgating by his truck with a brown paper bag. Bev's son was here now more days than not, too. After his parents divorced, after he failed all season to hit a ball out of the infield, after he struggled, according to Gus, the whole semester with pre-algebra, he had found his solace in the company of the lost boys. Stepping over a skull-covered skateboard, Jill heard her name.

"Hey Mrs. Oberdorf." The voice rose up past sepulcher eyes, limp bangs, a plume of smoke.

"Ian?"

He looked even smaller than she remembered, with the sort of fine, thin hands one admires in surgeons and calligraphers and harpists. Why did life refuse to behave like fiction? The puny guy who dropped every ball was supposed to be stellar at something else, at chess or cello or chiaroscuro; at identifying bugs, the stars, the planets, at which he would gaze beatifically each night enrapt. There was supposed to be one good, great thing, one Ian-y thing, and, in the end, a girl who would love him for it.

"Gus still playing ball?"

"Yes," she said. A breath, no more. Why was it that her son was born with a gift for the very thing he loved while Beatrix's son was left on the curb inhaling pork rinds and exhaust?

"Maybe I'll come up and watch him sometime."

How, if the Ians of the world were not given something comparable, could Jill stop at the corner store for the gallons of whole milk and the cases of protein bars Gus consumed in his quest to add heat to his fast ball with a clear conscience?

"Well, the season just ended."

"Oh, yeah. Right," he said and took a drag off his cigarette. "Maybe next year."

"That'd be good," Jill said, trusting that he'd never come, that he'd never know Gus had moved. That she'd lied to him. "Gus always liked having you on his teams, I know that."

"Yeah?" Ian dared her to meet his eyes, to confirm her deception.

With an awkward smile, she turned away. "Well..."

Ian flipped his board in the air so close to Jill's chin it nearly grazed her. Stepping back as if from a corpse, she cheeped, "Say hi to your mom for me."

Ian just shrugged. "Why?" he said, and planting his feet on a decal of blood, took off in a cacophonous haze.

Location, location, location.

What her son knew about setting up house could be written on a batting glove. It was one thing when it was just him, but now there were women and children to consider—neighborhoods, school districts, west-facing yards—but did Clem want her advice? Oh, no. Clem had it handled. Clem had it all figured out. Gabby pulled her arms tighter across her chest and checked her watch. There was no telling what sort of realtor he might have selected. Most likely some ex-ballplayer trying to eke out a living in the real world. When a sporty, gold sedan rounded the corner, Gabby rolled her eyes like a teenager.

"Morning, mom," Clem said. He stepped out of the passenger side, kissed his mother's cheek.

"You're late," Gabby sniped, and drawing from her repertoire of graceful contortions, wedged herself in the jump seat behind her leggy son.

Through the seat gap, a manicured hand appeared. "Karly La Mirada," the driver said.

"So glad you were able to join us today, Mrs. McGaffey."

Karly was a vision in salmon. Her pantsuit, her nails, her lips, her stilettos, all the same loud orange shade, a color that could only be worn with gold and lots of it. Her stiff blond hair was twisted in a showy chignon. Gabby didn't like the way she said *us*, or *today*, as if the two of them had been on some covert road trip for months. There was something in the air, and not just the residue of a half can of Aquanet. Tsunami qualms about the woman in orange showing up for Thanksgiving dinner in *Jill's seat* prompted Gabby to revert. "So, Ms. Mirada."

"La Mirada," Karly said, peeling out.

"Of course," Gabby said, her feet scrunched up against the center console. "So, how long have you and my son been working together?"

Karly placed her jeweled hand on Clem's forearm. "What has it been, Clem, three months?"

Gabby didn't like the sound of that one bit. She would have crossed her legs in disapproval but her son's seat was too far back.

"I got Karly's name from an ad," Clem said so cryptically Gabby feared it was the personals. "She specializes in the Hacienda Flats district."

Like a snap of a gum bubble, Karly interjected, "I've sold more homes in the HF than any broker in the Four Palms area."

"Oh," Gabby said, confused. "I didn't know you'd decided on any particular neighborhood."

"It's not the neighborhood, it's the school," Karly said.

"The schools are particularly good I take it?"

"The middle school's not much to speak of—" Karly confessed.

Clem turned back toward his mother, a configuration that amounted to her having a serious talk with the side of his face. "But he's only got one more year of middle school anyway, mom. It's high school that's important."

"Oh," Gabby said. "So I take it that the high school, then, has a good reputation."

Karly and Clem exchanged glances that once again made her leery of high-maintenance holidays. "Mom, Wilson High has the best baseball program in the state."

"My son graduated from Wilson two years ago," Karly said. "Now he's the starting pitcher at Tulane."

"Oh, how wonderful," Gabby said. "So, you're married?"

"Divorced."

Clem steered the conversation back on course. "The coach's name is Art Sanchez."

"He's been there twenty two years."

"Won the division title fifteen of them."

"Took the state title nine times."

"Has more former players on pro rosters than any coach in the Southwest."

Gabby tracked the resume points like a ping-pong ball. Apparently, it was Karly's turn. "No other realtor in Arizona has placed more varsity starters in the Wilson boundaries than yours truly." Turning her eye away from the highway upon which 18-wheelers passed blithely at 70 mph, Karly jangled a gold bracelet covered with charms: a bat, a ball, a little gold batting donut. "The team gave me this for all I've done to help with the recruiting program. They add a new charm each year."

"Gus won't find a more experienced coach between here and Phoenix."

"We had his stats faxed over last month," Karly said.

Gabby tried to envision a world where the batting average of a thirteen-year old boy would have any meaning at all. "To whom?"

"To my office," Karly said. "I'm very selective about who I work with." Again, she patted Clem's arm. "The team depends on it."

"Can you imagine if I had a chance to work with a coach like that in high school?"

So there it was, the mystery solved, the root source of her son's failure to achieve legendary status in the major leagues: Gabby's decision to place him a school where more kids could read than not. "Your high school coach was just fine."

"Well, Gus'll have better."

In the tight, squat, vibrating cubby where the AC didn't venture, Gabby's seat belt began to chafe. "It sounds like you've got it all figured out."

"Not really," Karly said. She eyed Gabby in the

rearview mirror like an ally in the war against clueless men. "Your son still hasn't told me how many bedrooms he's going to need."

The hard-earned creases between Gabby's brows popped like piqued antennae. "Clem?"

"What?"

"What do you mean, what? Haven't the two of you made some sort of a decision yet?" As tentative as they were with each other Gabby was amazed they'd ever been able to make a baby in the first place.

"Mom, this is between me and Jill, okay?"

Karly, acutely sensitive to the winds of vulnerable commissions, said, "If I might just make a suggestion. Three bedrooms, it seems to me, should give you all the options you need."

Clem turned his head away and, staring out at the blur of beige construction, offered his final word on the subject. "When it's right, we'll know it."

But whether he was referring to the house or the relationship, Gabby couldn't say.

Have yourself a merry little Christmas.

The last time snow fell on the stucco homes of the suburbs of Tucson, Arizona on Christmas Day was in 1933. Now, like a snow globe it swirled. Through every town and subdivision, along every luminary-lit path, from the tiny adobe parishes on the smudged outskirts of the city to the sandy edge of the far border of the dubiously prestigious Wilson High district, the whole of the town and all its minor characters were cast in a shimmery, white, transcendent glow.

Gabby hoisted the considerable turkey upon the table. "Ta-da!" It was twenty pounds easy, and glistened in that golden, brown crisp-skinned way that made mouths of all ages water.

Gus eyed the bird like a challenge. "Is there someone else coming?"

Gabby smiled. "Nope, just us."

"Well, let's hope for some hungry carolers later," Clem said.

Noting his grandmother's hand on her chair, Gus leapt to his feet. "Here, Gammy—" This, their compromise name. "Let me get that for you."

"Why thank you, young man. Your mother certainly did well by you in the manners department."

For a moment the three revelers fell silent. Clem

clutched the carving knife but could not bring himself to make the first cut. Turning to Gus, he said sternly, "Someone needs to call your mother."

Gus rose, once again, and with heavy, put-upon, dress-shoe steps, moved from the dining room table toward the staircase. "While it's still Christmas, buddy," Clem said. Gus made a fist, and seeking out a clearing on the wall between his yearly Sears portraits, he pounded with a shout. "Mo-om. Dinner!!"

On the other side of the wall, in a bookended version of this very room, Jill poured a thick, brown sauce into her mother's Wedgwood gravy boat. Wiping the lip clean, she set it on a small silver tray with an 0 engraved in the center. At the bottom of the stairs was an umbrella stand. Jill grabbed a wooden bat and tapped three times in response.

"Coming!" A framed photo of Eudora Welty's study tipped askew in the transaction. Jill carefully-righted it before heading out.

From door to door, the journey took eight steps. Jill straddled the flocked sagebrush border between their two units, and entered knocking, infusing the air with the sweet-salt smells of steaming gravy. "Merry Christmas," she beamed. "Again."

The four of them had already had coffee cake and juice over the opening of gifts, the ratio of which was an embarrassing 24-to-1 in Gus's favor. There were baseball shirts and pants and calendars. There were new cleats and old trading cards. There were pine tar rags and weighted bat donuts and a rebound net for fielding practice. There was a new aluminum bat for power and two wooden ones for training in the off-season. There was a boxed set of Dos Passos' *USA Trilogy* which Gus actually took from its shrinkwrap, reading aloud from the jacket for at least a minute and a half. There was a CD from Gabby with Native Southwest tribal music— "thanks, Gammy, sounds neat," Gus had managed to say convincingly.

Clem had given Jill a lovely silver necklace with a turquoise pendant. She, an original recording of "Whose on First?" over which they all laughed to the point of tears, Gus, most of all.

"Sorry I'm late," Jill said, "But I didn't think the meal would be complete without this."

She set the silver tray on the table. "Mole sauce. A McGaffey/Oberdorf family tradition."

Gus's nose wrinkled up like a St. Bernard's. "Mole sauce? On Turkey??"

"It's a long story," Gabby said, and with bright, grateful eyes, patted the back of the empty chair.

After the meal was finished and the dishes were cleaned and Gus was wholly preoccupied with some simulated universe on the screen, Gabby brought out one last gift. With a whisper she called Clem and Jill close. "Just a little something. For old time's sake," she said and held out a large, gold-foiled envelope. Inside, was a certificate for a weekend getaway at the hotel where they had last been together as a couple, the hotel where Gus, if any of them cared to think about it, was obviously conceived. They had gotten too comfortable as friends for Gabby's taste. What they needed was a little nudge. "I'll babysit, of course."

Clem looked at Jill. "You could use a weekend away."

Jill demurred. "So could you."

"If you don't go together, I'm taking it back."

Clem blushed and slipped the gift in his pocket. "I'm sure we can figure something out."

They decided to go on the third weekend in January. On Friday morning, they packed their bags in their separate homes and set them out on their separate stoops.

"Ready?" Clem said.

"Yep." Jill smiled.

They were already in the car, alone, together, inches away, for the first time in forever. Jill just needed to check the toaster oven. She was in the kitchen when the phone rang. Had she not been there to answer it, the school would have called the next name on the list, the grandmother, to inform her that Gus was feverish and hurling.

"Go, please. He'll be fine," Gabby said, upon hearing of their plans to stay home with Gus, but neither of them seemed to consider it.

Over the next two weeks, the stomach bug traveled

back and forth across the duplex. By the time Clem and Jill were ready to try again, it was Valentine's Day, and there was no room at the inn.

"Maybe next month" Clem said.

"Yeah," Jill said and patted his hand. They both knew better. By the middle of February the baseball season had started to overtake every part of the house. Every part except one. The one small room on the side where Jill lived, where silently, secretly, in a way that consumed her beyond the point of needing any escape at all, she was chipping away at what was starting to seem—shapeless, formless, titleless blob that is was—like her real work.

Breakthrough.

Jill's writing time was now inviolable. She had one whole free weekday and two whole free mornings, and with more people to meet Gus's needs than she knew what to do with, sometimes even whole errand-free stretches on the weekends. There were no stupors of inspiration. The words came in fits and starts, moaning themselves into being one heel-dragging letter at a time. A hundred pages into a draft of a novel, and still she had no idea what she was writing. No matter. With a child's stubborn fealty, Jill bowed her head at the allotted hour, typing and humming and taking her feckless pokes at the truth, and waited tenaciously for the answers to come.

And so it was, on a certain day in May, when the first of the Saguaro blossoms were in bloom and the spring air was so soft to the cheek it was as if it had no temperature at all, the words began to come in whole gulping pages, in chapters, in lives, characters bursting full-blown before Jill's bifocaled eyes faster than she could get it down on the—

"Mo-om!"

During seminal stages of creation all unessential senses were shut down. Her ears, in this moment, were frivolous.

"Mo-om!!" She felt, more than heard, the rumble of feet on the stairs. Two, then four. Jill bore down on the keys, typing as if her very life depended on the retention of the next—

"Ohgoodyou'rehereguesswhat?" Gus said, all one word.

Jill lifted a hand: HALT. She could feel them in the doorway, impatient, amused. Type on, Jill Oberdorf, type on. Only when she sensed motion approaching, breath on her neck, eyes on her page, did she hit the save button and clear the screen. Swiveling abruptly, she said like a blade in the air, "What's up?"

"Is this a bad time?" Clem asked.

"Not anymore." Her tight smile quickly softened at the sight of her son, of Clem. "So, c'mon tell me. What's the big news?"

"Dad took me by Wilson on the way home from school."

"Thought it would be a good idea for him to meet Coach Sanchez ahead of time."

"He invited me to work out with the team for the day."

"When?"

"Today."

"I brought clothes for him, just in case," Clem explained.

Jill studied Gus's red face, his muddy pants, the subtle melon dusk light through the shades. "What time is it?"

"6:30," Clem said.

Jill turned to the clock to verify. "Oh my gosh." She took note of her lap, her pajamas, the crumbs of the toast she'd eaten sometime that day. Cupping her hand to her mouth, she exhaled. "Um, yeah. Gosh, I don't know where the day went," she said, and threading the boys, ducked into the bathroom. "Sorry I'm looking so..."

"Deranged?" said Gus.

"Good word," said Jill.

"You look just fine," Clem said. "A little consumed, that's all."

Jill smiled and shoved a toothbrush in her mouth. "So, tell me everything."

"It was awesome, mom. I mean, really tough. We ran, we did squats, we did long toss all the way across the outfield. Wait till you see the arms on these kids— every one of them's got a gun. I'm telling you, I don't think I'm going to be able to move tomorrow."

With a mouth full of paste suds, she mumbled. "An ou ure its not too uch?"

"He did great," Clem said. "He definitely held his own."

"Roolly?" she said and spit. Her mousy brown, no-longer-styled hair stuck out in nestlike tufts and spikes. And was that sleep in her eyes? Dousing her face with water, Jill rinsed, blotted.

"And that's not even the exciting part," Clem said.

"Coach Sanchez wants me to workout with the team this summer."

"You're kidding." Gus hadn't even started high school

yet. "This summer?"

"Just think of it, Jilly," Clem said with a wink. "Night games from June to Labor Day."

Like a sigh it all came flooding back. Night games was not a word, not even two, but an epic poem of the sweetest chapter of her young life. She could see it now, the glowing green, the inky sky, the white-hot lights making it all seem like something out of a movie. Goose pimples rose up along her bare arms as she recalled the feel of the warm winds, cold beers, of the echo of coyotes in the teasing 0-and-2 silence, and afterwards, the exultant howls spilling out unabashedly through her thrown-open dorm room window.

Jill looked at her son, whose Adam's apple was bobbing eagerly in his throat and said, once again, as if she could stop it. "This summer?"

Go Bobcats.

Jill's imagination had gotten ahead of itself. Being the mother of a bench-warming pre-rookie in a high school summer league was about as far from the heat as a body could get. No one asked her name or the name of her son. No one said welcome or told her where she might get one of the green and gold Bobcat t-shirts they all seemed to be wearing. At Gus's first appearance on the field—a beeline past the fence to fetch a foul ball—no one approached fawningly and said, "Ooo, he's good."

But it was Clem that she'd misread the most, mistaking his happiness for the absence of pain. Turning to him for reassurance, Jill saw in his numb and restless eyes that he was in no position to offer her anything but a front row view of the firsthand anguish of what screening nightly reruns of what should have been can do to a man. Without a word he rose, drifted. Ex-ballplaying dads didn't sit, they stood, if not in the dugout, then along the outfield fence, at a distance commensurate with their own success.

Jill turned to Gabby who was bent over a needlepoint sampler, blithe and unperturbed, as a boy with arms as thick as Gus's thighs pointed, without compunction, his fanged metal cleats into the rib of an awaiting infielder.

"Is he a senior?" Jill inquired timidly of the nearest

268

Bobcat mom.

"Randolph? No. Sophomore."

Again, Jill revised her list, her standard. What chance did her son have against these boys, these men; men who drove cars and had girlfriends and were, no doubt, teaching Gus all sorts of bad words as she sat idly by in the stands. What was it, she struggled now to recall, that she used to love so much about sitting outside on an inhospitable plank of tin watching other people's children play games in the dark?

Combatting pessimism, she cried out, "Here we go Landeros!"

Her cheer was greeted like a heckler at church. It was not until the batter got on base that Jill realized his name was Buchard.

Behind a green-tarped cage that led from the dugout to the batter's box, it was possible to check for shadows, silhouettes, hints of familiar profiles through the cracks where the thick sheets of mesh failed to meet. In the bottom of the seventh inning, a figure looking very much like her son but larger, more formidable, moved in shadows behind the green scrim. She could sense him taking practice swings, feel his earnestness, his feigned cool. Jill clutched Gabby's hand to still it, and together they watched as Gus stepped into the chalked box for his first official Bobcat at bat.

"Who's that?" someone asked.

"Anyone got a name on this kid?"

Gabby slid her needle into a stopping square and casually scratched her nose. "I think it's Oberdorf."

Jill turned toward the curious stands and made a correction. "Actually, it's McGaffey."

To Gabby's questioning brow, she explained. "Sounds better over a P.A. don't you think?"

Jill had seen fast pitching before but not in years, and never in front of her own flesh and bones.

The pitcher was throwing 100 mph easy; maybe two. Gus swung so hard on the first pitch he nearly knocked himself down. Mortification was tempered by mercy.

"All we need is a base hit, kid!"

"C'mon McGaffey, just make contact."

Suddenly, her son had a name and a place. The pitcher threw low and Gus held back for 1 and 1. "Alright McGaffey, way to be smart up there!" The third pitch curved clean and mean. Gus swung and stumbled.

"Don't let him mess with you McGaffey!"

"Gotta protect up there"

"C'mon rook, let's keep it alive."

The next pitch was low and outside. Gus fouled it away.

"Way to battle, McGaffey!"

He fouled off the next pitch. And the next, sending one soaring so high and so far that it grazed his father's cheek just over the deep left field fence.

"Here we go now, next one's yours!"

And the next. And the next.

Seven foul balls later, Gus's face flushed and beaded, the imprint of Jill's nails branded into Gabby's hand, his efforts were rewarded with an impotent little nubber that went straight into the pitcher's glove for the final, anticlimactic out of the game.

No one groaned. Streaming out across the field, the Wilson High boys huddled around the coach, Gus no less a part of the whole than the other thirty boys who lifted their fists as one in the center to shout, "One, two, three. Bobcats!" He was not the smallest or the thinnest or even the farthest from the center.

"Your boy's gonna be good," a woman said in passing— a saint of a woman, a Bobcat mom.

"Thanks," Jill said and beamed like a bottle rocket. "Which one's your son?"

"Oh, I don't have a player on the team anymore," the woman replied. "I'm Nora Sanchez. The coach's wife."

Legumes.

If Gus had shown up on her doorstep with a butterfly net or a tuba or, God forbid, a basketball, Gabby wasn't entirely sure she'd have known what to do with him. As it was, their Sundays together were effortless, familiar but unfettered by the burden of parental anxiety. She could help him, to be sure, but whether he took her up on her offers, this would be entirely up to him. Steering the grocery cart past the section where the dried peas and beans were stacked in ten-pound bags, Gabby said offhandedly, "Did I ever tell you that I used to pitch beans to your dad for batting practice?"

Gus put his hand on the cart to stop it. "Did it help?"

"Did it help?" she replied with rhetorical glee. "The first season we tried it—he was in a slump—three weeks later he was batting .413."

Gus studied the colorful shelves of legumes like a seating chart at a major league ballpark. Running his hand up and down the lumpy edges of the cellophane bags, he asked, "What kind did dad use?"

"Your dad was a pinto bean man."

The pintos were on the top shelf with the Great Northerns and the kidneys and the other larger beans. Tracing his finger downward, Gus fixed his mind on the bottom. "How 'bout these?"

"Lentils?" Gabby said, furrowing. "I think those are going to be a little too small."

Apparently that was all Gus needed to hear. Stacking four bags in the cart he said with a cocksure grin, "Yeah, but if I can see these coming, I can see anything."

Welcome to Wilson High.

Registration for the fall semester took place the week before Labor Day. It was easy to tell the freshman. They were the only ones with parents in tow. The older students arrived in groups and gangs and couplets, slouching in amorphous, ragtag lines behind their proscribed windows. In line L-R, Jill and Gus inched their way forward, finally arriving at the dusty, backlit screen.

"Gus McGaffey," he said, as if still expecting someone to question the name.

Jill stood beside her son fighting the urge to lean in and spell it.

"Here we go," the woman said. She could have been any teacher on any high school campus in America. Doe-eyed and dew-skinned and ready to change the world she had arrived, and now, facing menopause and her own limitations, had nothing left in her to glisten with. "Check it over, see if everything looks right."

"No," Gus said. Before Jill could sneak a glimpse over his shoulder, he continued, "This is wrong." His voice began to crack as he turned to his mom. "I'm supposed to be in baseball conditioning 6th period. All the JV players are in that class."

"Excuse me," Jill said, leaning in through the window. "But my son's supposed to be in the baseball conditioning class

6th period. It was all arranged this summer."

The woman scrutinized the form, slid it back through the window. "Well, it looks like he's in first period conditioning instead."

"Well," Jill said, sliding the card back, "Someone's going to have to change it. He needs to be with the team."

"I don't think you understand." The woman returned the blue card once more. "He is with the team. First period conditioning is for the varsity.

Jill could feel Gus's body go stock still beside her. "The varsity?"

"Your son must be a very good player."

"Are you sure there's not some mistake?"

"No one gets put in that class without Coach Sanchez' permission."

Forget last names. The signs over the registration windows should have read, in clear and descending order: Destiny Yours, Bright Future, Biding Time, Hanging In, Last Chance. Wasn't high school, after all, where the first cruel cuts were made?

"Excuse us," Jill said, and forging their way back through the crowd, through the thickets of red eyes and ill-fitting pants, past the girl with the baby stroller, the boy with the chains that hung menacingly from his belt loops, past libidinous land mines and the mob's base sway, guided her son away from the pack.

All hallow's eve.

Jill wanted it to be the best Halloween ever. She put everything else aside—writing, grading—and sought to rekindle in this dry and seasonless land, the autumnal visions of her childhood. From a displaced maple on the shady side of campus, she gathered two trash bags of fallen leaves, crimson and rust and gold, and scattered them like a whirlwind across the yard. She ironed her mother's cornucopia linens and piled high upon them a display of squash and Indian corn. She roasted the seeds from the pumpkins they'd carved, making manifest with their slimy, playful hands three goofy, toothless faces which now waited on the stoop for nightfall. She lined the walkway that led to Clem's door with brown, whole-punched bags weighed down with sand and illuminated with squat, orange votives. There. Jill smiled as she lit the last of them and, ignoring the gruesome deathfest of effigies and tombstones in the yards on either side of her, walked back up the step, past the scarecrow on the hay bale, beneath the glowey orange garland of candy corn lights, to check the pumpkin pies.

There was a dismal thump in the hall. Lifting her head from the oven, she saw in the doorway, beneath a purple-foiled BOO!, her ashen son.

"Gussy?" she said, sliding the pies on the cooling rack.

"What is it?"

"Coach Sanchez quit."

"What?"

"They offered him a job over at Arizona State," Gus said and fell in a heap on the couch. "He starts next week."

Jill slid the oven mitts off her hands and struggled for bearings: the earth was round, the stars were innumerable, and Gus was going to play four years of varsity ball for the best coach in the state. "I don't understand?" Tiny needles began to tap at her forehead. "How can he just leave like this in the middle of the year?"

"I don't know. He said that's when it happens, in the preseason."

She scanned the room as if trying to assess the damage of the blast from the remains. Zeroing in on her son's dropped duffel, she asked warily, "What about conditioning?"

"There won't be any till they find a new coach."

"Well, do they have any candidates?"

"Mo-om, he just quit today!"

Their town, their neighborhood, their unlikely duplex, all had been chosen so that Gus could play for Coach Sanchez; he was the tablecloth beneath their new life, and now, by some cruel and dexterous magic, had been pulled out from under them. Jill did not endeavor a solution. Wiping her hands on her mother's apron, she said as if it were a habit as old as time, "I'm calling your father."

Trick-or-treat.

In a matter of hours, the topsy-turvy world seemed, like a punching clown, to have righted itself. The candy bowl was running low but the redemptive power of the best Halloween ever was positively brimming. Jill's homemade corn tamale casserole had been a huge success; Clem had two helpings. Gus, who, only hours before had lain exsanguinated on the sofa, was now shaping smiley faces on fat wedges of pumpkin pie with the spray nozzle of Redi-Whip. By the time Gabby arrived, Jill and Clem and Gus were nearly looking back on the events of the day and laughing.

Gabby let herself in. "I don't even know why I bother. Two trick-or-treaters. That's how many I had. Two kids in three hours."

"That's too bad, mom," Clem said with a butterscotch grin.

"We've had all kinds of action here," Gus snickered.

"Have some pie. You'll feel better," Jill said, as if it were the punch line to a joke.

Gabby folded her arms. "Alright, what'd I miss?"

Tipping the can of whipped cream in his mouth Gus swirled it full and sputtered, "Just everything."

The doorbell rang. Jill leapt to answer it, offering Gabby an affectionate squeeze in passing. "Don't tell her till I get back."

"Tell me what?"

"Try the pie, mom," Clem said, positioning a slice closer. "Jill made it herself."

"I don't want any pie, thank you. Now will someone, please—"

At the front door, Jill took her own, sweet time—"are you a bear? a fox? oh, a ferret, of course"—while at the table, Clem and Gus set kernels of candy corn in their spoons and, flipping them up under pounded fists, gulped at the air.

"You two are really enjoying this, aren't you?" Gabby said stiffly.

"Alright," Jill returned. "What'd I miss?"

"We were trying to decide whether to tell mom the good news or the bad news first."

"Oh, I'd say the bad news," Jill suggested.

"Who cares about the bad news," Gus said, "Let's just tell her the good news."

"Oh for heaven's sakes, somebody tell me something quick or I'm leaving."

"Coach Sanchez quit today."

"What?" Gabby gripped the lip of the table. The earth was made in seven days. The freezing point of water was 32 degrees. And the suffering of her only son would be redeemed in her grandson. "How can he do that? It's the middle of the school year?"

"That's what I said, but wait. Here's the good news."

The doorbell rang again. This time it was Gus who jumped up. "Wait till I get back."

"Don't ask for their life story," Gabby snapped. "Just give them the candy and get back here!"

In his absence Gabby tapped her fork against Jill's mother's dessert plates till she nearly chipped the gilded edge. "Did you know about this?" she asked Clem.

He shook his head cluelessly until Gus returned and Jill began, "So, the good news is—"

"The good news is," Gus interrupted, "that on Monday morning, Dad is going to go down to the school to tell them he'll take the job."

"It's not like I'm running the show at U of A, anyway," Clem explained. "And besides, how often does a father get to coach his own kid? Reaching over to squeeze Gus's arm he said, "I'm going to get this guy so ready for college, the scouts won't know what hit 'em."

"How many high schools get to have a real pro as their coach?" Jill said. "Sanchez never even got drafted."

"Yeah. Forget the state title. We're going all the way," Gus chimed.

"Well, let's not get ahead of ourselves, buddy."

In the same way that only moments before she had stood on the outside of their common delight, Gabby was again alone. "Gammy, what's wrong?"

"It's a wonderful idea, Gus. It really is..."

"But?" Clem pressed.

"Yeah, but?" Gus refrained.

Was it possible that he had forgotten? Had allowed himself to forget. Gabby watched her son's eyes for a dawning, saw it come instead on the face of her grandson's mother.

Jill took a pragmatic breath. "But you can't coach a high school team without a degree."

Pointlessly, Gabby added, "We went over all this years ago."

"What are you talking about?" Gus said. "Dad went to U of A. That's where you two met."

Clem sat back, tossed his orange napkin on the plate. "I left after my junior year, Gus. The Dodgers drafted me in the second round. I figured that was the end of needing a fall back plan."

Once again, the bell rang. No one moved; not Gus who was busy declaring the truth unfair, or Gabby who was pained to concur, or Clem who picked silently at a loose thread in the embroidered cloth. Jill shoved her chair back so hard it toppled. Smarties sloshing up the lip of the candy bowl, she shouted to no one present, "Enough already!" and reached with an indignant hand for the door.

Impotence.

Under the tacit division of domestic labor, it seemed to Jill that all baseball-related decisions would best be left to Clem, but by January she was having second thoughts. First there was the matter of the new varsity coach, a ruddy, bulbous-nosed man whose primary credential was that he'd taught health at Wilson for the past twenty years. Both of his sons had ridden the bench for Coach Sanchez, and were now, if rumors were to be trusted, forging bright futures selling pot in an alley off a side street that fed in and out of Wilson High. And what did Clem have to say about that?

"A good player can always rise above a bad coach." As if the sky weren't falling. As if it were out of his hands. When, on the last day of the winter semester, Gus came home with a skimpy, cotton JV jersey and a spring schedule that no longer referred to him as a member of the varsity, Clem had merely sighed under the invisible weight of some irrefutable truth and said, "That's baseball."

Maybe he was right. Maybe he was trying to teach Gus an important lesson. Maybe Gus'd go on to be a better ballplayer, a better man, for the experience. Or maybe, Jill thought as she teetered across the grass in heels she wore almost as rarely as a short skirt with nylons, Clem simply no longer had it in him to fight.

"Yoo-hoo! Excuse me, Coach Eichler?" Jill made sure to place the emphasis on the title. "I'm so sorry to bother you while you're working with the team, but I think maybe there's been a mistake. I'm hoping you can clear it up for me." Eichler gripped the fence and said nothing. "Well," Jill continued, "as you know the new schedules were handed out yesterday. My son's said something about him being in the JV group." Jill was just about to tell him Gus's name when he cut her off.

"That's right," he said to the fence. "Freshmen play JV. That's how a high school program's supposed to be run and that's how I intend to run it."

Eichler's mottled cheek was like a starfish at red tide. Jill tried to overlook the pain that would lead to as many burst blood vessels as that, as she continued. "Well, as a general rule, I would certainly agree with you. But for every rule there is an exception."

"You've obviously never been in the military," he quipped, pleased.

Jill tapped at the fence wire as if to delete the start of the scene, insert a new tack. "But I'm sure over the years you've seen certain players..." Even as she said it she began to wonder if Gus was really one of them. Was he really that much better than the other freshmen, or, as the autumn whispers had claimed, was Coach Sanchez simply trying to secure the cache of Clem's involvement.

"Lady," he said, turning at last to face her. His breath

stank of cheap scotch and wintergreen. It seemed in that moment that he knew she would come, that it was him, and not Jill, that was writing the scene. "If I had a dime for every mom who thought her kid was the greatest thing since sliced bread I wouldn't need to hang around this dump."

"But Coach Sanchez—"

"You see Coach Sanchez around here? No. Me neither. That's because Coach Sanchez wasn't interested in anything but making a name for himself. He didn't care about these kids. He didn't care about this school." The varsity squad ran past them in a warm-up lap. "How 'bout a little hustle you faggots!" Without missing a beat he continued. "Sanchez ran around here like this was some sort of training camp for the pros. Hurt a lot of good kids in the process. You think your kid's got talent?" Eichler lowered his sunglasses, revealed two watery gray eyes trapped beneath a milky, yellow film. "My boys had more talent than anyone that every played at this school. Could have gone anywhere. Could have played at U of A, even. But your buddy Sanchez killed any chance of that. The oldest one, he gave his spot to some 15-year-old spic. Sat my kid on the bench all year. The youngest one, he cut him after the first day of tryouts, and he was the only one on the whole goddamn field getting the job done. I was here. I saw it. So here's how it's going to be on my watch. Seniors who don't give me any lip start, and if there's any spots left I'm giving them to the juniors, and all the rest of them can just wait their turn."

Walking back across the football field to her car, Jill grew increasingly sure footed. Eichler would be a temporary setback, a blip in the narrative. A character like him could not help but self-destruct. By the end of the season, he'll have choked someone— a player or a parent or an ump. He'll have called the wrong person the wrong name. He'll have passed out in his own vomit in a heap by the chalker. Any other turn of events would simply lack realism.

Except, Jill frowned as she stumbled in a divot on the patchy grass, in the looking-glass bureaucracy of the school system that had hired him.

Making adjustments.

Clem had played a double header once with three cleats missing on each shoe. He had pitched with a borrowed first baseman's glove. With blood blisters. On fields with no mound, with no rubber; with a mound and a rubber so high he almost fell off it each time he made a pick-off throw. He had played with catchers who knew more about the game than he did and rookies who couldn't remember the signs. He had played on fields with backstops so deep that every passed ball was a run, and backstops so short he had to struggle with the impetus to be precise. He had played before great umps and drunk umps and fair umps and umps on the take. He had been called in to close, to relieve, to start, to sit. He had batted leadoff and cleanup and ninth. He had, at every turn, at every moment of his no-longer young life, done what was required to reach the elusive goal. If that meant returning to a full-time courseload of every class he'd put off at the age of 21—Trig and Poli-Sci and the History of Art from the Stone Age to the Renaissance— well then, by God, if for no other reason than to show Gus it could be done, he'd make that adjustment, too. Jill had watched the decision in progress, watched the gears turn and the forces galvanize and the spirit hoist itself from low ebb of the sofa cushions.

In the driveway now, she honked. Clem raced, coffee

sloshing, out to the car and dropped his backpack at the foot of the passenger seat.

"Got your homework?" Jill asked.

"You're really enjoying this, aren't you?"

"Yes, I am," she said and gazed at him in a wholly unacademic way.

"Me, too."

Cut off from the world, alone, together, they could have sat there all morning. Would have. Should have.

"We better go," Clem said, eyeing the clock.

"Yep," Jill nodded, and burying a smile in the side mirror, said, "Buckle up."

Coach Woo.

He had not been strong enough to make the leap, at thirteen, from the little league to the senior field, but Darryl Woo knew baseball. He could recount from memory the stats of every player in the Major Leagues, active and retired. He could recap, inning by inning, every game of every World Series for the past thirty years, and the moment at which the games had turned. He had declined, three times, the Chair of the Wilson High math department so that the second half of his day could be spent grooming the JV baseball team. He had no children. Coach Woo's legacy was the mounting list of boys who'd moved from the JV to the Varsity and then on to college where they'd declared with a statistically-small-but-significant frequency, a major in mathematics.

On the eve of the JV season, Coach Woo announced in a parents' meeting that he'd like to do even better. Jill, feeling with a g-force urgency that whatever it was she was trying to write was not nearly as important as whatever it was he was trying to do, raised her hand like a sparkler to help. The following week a trailer arrived, a donation from an anonymous citizen. Shortly thereafter, they began to convene in this makeshift study hall, Coach Woo and the players who wanted to work, and Jill, who, arrived each afternoon bearing foiled half-trays of enchiladas and pizza and ginger beef—a grant of leftovers from the U of A cafeteria—and piled the plates of the ravenous boys with good things.

"How'd we do in Geography this week, Dennis?"

"Ah, Mrs. 0. Why do I need to know where all these places are? No one in my family's ever left Arizona."

"Maybe because they didn't know there was anywhere else to go," Jill said holding back a brownie. "You're going to bring me a B next week, right?"

"A B?" Dennis protested.

"You're right," Jill said. "You can do better than that. Bring me an A, or no enchiladas."

A pained voice cried out from the study table. "Coach Woo?!!"

The boys, who were flung across beds, across ledges, atop counters where no amount of 409 had been able to remove the dried yolk, turned to find that the face looking up glazed from the math text belonged to Gus's dad. "I know you just showed me, but..."

As if Coach Woo had no doubt that the aha! was inevitable for those who persisted, he hurdled the sea of legs to Clem's side. "Let's see where the trouble is..."

Across the cramped table Gus mashed his pen in frantic strokes and feverishly shouted, "I'm done!"

The competitive spirit was no less alive here than on the field. Being first to shut the books was considered, in the early weeks of their time together, the academic equivalent of a grand slam. But by mid-spring, the place of honor slowly shifted to the boy who could bear to study the longest. Double-checking became a process no less ridiculous than backing up a play. Making the out meant no mistakes.

"Oo, Coach McGaffey, that looks a lil' sloppy. I don't know if we gonna let you come take b.p on Sunday," Ramon teased.

If not scholarship, precisely, then something like pride in the mastery of the task began to seep into the agile, peripatetic boys who were rewarded for weekly grade goals with a Sunday afternoon road trip. Dogpiling into Clem's Expedition (are you sure there's enough belts for everyone? Jill frowned) they headed off to the U of A field, an incentive that had less to do with the practice of batting than with the instilling of the idea that they belonged there.

Commencement.

By June, all the seniors were gone and with them, the memory of Coach Eichler. En route to the first round of the district play-offs he flipped his car on the freeway. His body was found in the weeds 100 feet away. With a blood alcohol level of 2.3, it was said that his death would have been painless. There were three players riding in the car with him— all of them juniors. One died at the scene, another shattered seven bones and spent a year in traction. The third merely went into a sort of ambulatory shock. During summer league games, which Clem and Coach Woo quickly stepped in to organize, Jill thought she saw him in the shadows of the outfield, a cigarette like a flare in his small, nervous lips.

Growing pains.

By his 15th birthday Gus had reached the six-foot mark. He and Dennis, a rising junior, were the tallest of the new crop, a fact that seemed to be growing more noticeable by the day. "All the men in my family get their spurts late," the second baseman's mom proclaimed nervously one night without prompting.

"Middle infielders don't need to be huge," Jill offered as reassurance.

"Oh, no," the mother said emphatically, glaring at her son as if willing him to grow, "The doctor assures us he'll be 6' 2." His stubble was so heavy Jill could see it from the bleachers. Only a mother could believe he had another eight inches laying dormant in his seventeen-year old genes.

All Jill could say was, "Really?" before an opposing batter hit a line drive straight up the middle and silenced them both. In defiance of the laws of gravity and human limitations, Rufino Morales leapt from short to snag it midair and, with nothing but three ribs to support him, gunned the ball to first for the out. Second only to the joy of anything Gus, was the thrill of a great infield snag. This Jill could see. This Jill could appreciate. Somehow the fact that she understood everything there was to understand about the play, and the boy who made it, made her cheer louder for him than for anyone else on the

Wilson team.

"No one but Rufino could have made that play," Jill beamed, crooking her head towards Mr. Morales, who stood off to the side like a visitor. His grateful smile was bittersweet. On the family tree from which Rufino Morales had taken root there was not a single person over 5' 3." For him there were no delusions of grandeur; there would be no college teams, no major league dreams. In the straw draw of destiny, the greatest young infielder Jill had ever seen had simply come up short.

I don't believe we've met.

Not the words of Blake or Tolstoy or Dickinson, not Ode to Joy or an infant's drooly grin or the rousing hollow beneath Clem's raised arm— nothing stirred Jill more than the sight of her own son poised in the stretch, his arm folded behind his back as if to conceal a winning hand. His body no longer seemed a part of anything as small as Jill but rather, as he planted his feet on the mound, that God himself had cast him there in that bronze-worthy pose for His own good pleasure.

With the same unsettling confidence that had buoyed his assertion at the age of five that his life's calling was to do just this, Gus stood beneath the white lights and the August moon, and surreptitiously scanned the perimeter. The pick-off at first seemed an impossible task. Pointless, even. The odds of a ball going wild were, in Jill's humble opinion, far greater than ever beating the runner to the bag. And besides, how many things was a single player expected to keep track of?

She had asked many times for a risk/benefit analysis of the maddening play. Had listened and nodded much the same way that Gus did (Clem, too, come to think of it), whenever Jill tried to explain the imagery in a literary text. ("Don't you see how it's really just a metaphor for the isolation and despair the capitalist machine breeds in the soul of man?") *Oh, I get it now*, they would say but even if, in that moment they meant it, the insight failed to penetrate.

Even after all these years, Jill's appreciation of the game was limited to what she could see. She could see the ball leave the hand of a pitcher. She could see it cross the plate. She could tell if it was high or low, (but not if it was inside or out). She recognized a change-up now and, more often than not, a curve (she felt she deserved some credit for this). She could tell if the batter hit the ball and if a fielder caught or dropped it. If he dropped it, which happened much less frequently in high school, there was usually time to scan back to the infield to assess the damage. But as for simultaneously watching a batter and a base runner, or trying to steal signs, or anticipating a bunt or a certain pitch—forget it. Up and down the bleachers the fans would murmur "hit n' run" (how did they know? Was there a message flashed on the scoreboard?) and Jill would nod as if she were in on it when, in fact, what she really wanted to say was "Isn't hitting and running always the idea?"

Gus threw a fast ball straight down the center. She had expected his arm to tire this late in the season but it had not; just the week before Clem had clocked him at 79 mph. By his senior year, he would be throwing at that plus ten. Returning to the stretch, feline and scanning, Gus again snapped the ball to first.

"Forget about the runner, for chrissakes! Just get the batter!!"

The stranger's coarse remonstration came from behind Jill's right shoulder. She didn't know which she hated more, the sound of his voice or the fact that she couldn't say for certain whether or not he was right. Maybe she understood more than she knew. Maybe the pickoff was a waste of time. Again, the runner teased, and again, Gus bit.

"Jesus H. Christ, pitcher. Just take care of business at the plate!"

What happened next, Jill couldn't really say. She was watching Gus throw the ball to the catcher when—

"He's going!! HE'S GOING!! For chrissakes! The runner is going!!" The ball was already out of Gus's hand. A slight hitch in his release point made it cross the plate in the dirt, turning one stolen base quickly into two. "Jesus Christ!! " the stranger shouted, slapping his hands on his thighs like a bullwhip.

As a rule Jill found it unwise to engage other parents in contention. Seasons were too long, the seats too close together. Splaying her hand upon her knee for ballast, she turned, slowly, cooly, controlling her voice like a split-fingered fastball. "He can concentrate on the base runner, or he can concentrate on the batter. Good as he is, he can't do both." Eye to eye with the hairy white belly that spilled out from under the voice's stretched and faded t-shirt, Jill felt as if she'd won a great victory for rational thought.

The man sneered and, gathering a cheekful of seed spit,

unloaded through the cracks in the bleacher slats. "Well he better learn to. My boy's only got one more year. Someone's gonna need to step up."

Jill had never seen the man before. The fact that he had a son on the team he presumed to be the starting pitcher was like hearing about a child you never knew you had. "I'm sorry, who are you?"

The man pointed his chin toward the bullpen. There in the shadows on the side of the field, she saw on the mound in a Wilson jersey a boy who looked like two Gusses stuck together. He was built like a bag of catcher's gear, dense and lumpy and in every way unsuitable for bronzing. "I'm Turk's dad. Turk Hostler. Threw 87 miles an hour this summer for his travel club. 2.47 ERA in the regular season. Has a real good feel for the pickoff."

Jill knew all about Turk Hostler. She'd been at the meeting when Clem and Coach Woo had reviewed the year-end stats. Eichler's legacy of seniority and drunkenness had left the Wilson varsity with only two returning starters, only one of them, a pitcher. A pitcher whose 2.47 ERA was based on a grand total of three innings in which he'd picked off precisely no one.

On the field, Gus threw a pitch that caused the batter to fall to his knees in an effort to hit it, and the scoreless inning was over.

"Way to go, pitch. Way to hang tough in a jam!"

Suddenly, Turk's dad was Gus's biggest fan. Proffering his open seed bag to Jill, he said by way of a chat, "You heard about Coach Eichler, of course?"

"Yes. It's a terrible thing."

"A real loss," he said. "The kids really liked him." Jill placed a seed in the center of her two front teeth and bit down. "Buddy of mine knows a guy who was at the scene, says Eichler wasn't even the one driving. It was one of the kids. Only they won't cop to it."

Like kaleidoscope fragments, alternative scenarios came into focus, one after another, and each casting Coach Eichler in a rosier light than the next. Just like that, the carefree nights of summer were over, intruded upon by the boney poke that left on a willing soul the bruises of wisdom. All Jill had wanted was a simple story: good guys and bad guys, heroes and villains, winners and losers.

Making his way down the bleachers Turk's dad turned back and smiled. "Get ya anything from the snack bar?"

It was then that she noticed he was missing a tooth. "No thanks," Jill said. Breezily she added, as if to reassure herself, "I'm good."

Mom and dad.

In any other house the image of a mother and a father recounting the events of the day over a glass of wine after the children had gone to bed would be utterly unspectacular. Jill had never felt so ordinary in all her life.

"Well, I think I'll go to sleep now," Gus said.

"Alright, buddy," Clem replied.

"Good game tonight," Jill added. "You were really working those base runners."

"Thanks," Gus said, hesitating on the bottom stair. "So, are you guys just going to watch a movie or something?"

"I don't think so," Clem said.

"No, it's kind of late." Jill curled her knees up on the couch. "See you in the morning."

Outside the moon shone through the skylight like a spot from on high. Clem refilled their glasses, searched his limited collection for a suitable CD.

In lieu of *I better go*, Jill said, "So, there's a girl in my Advanced Comp class. I found out today she lives in my old dorm room. Our old dorm room. She wrote a poem for class, "Ode to Room 432."

"No way," Clem smiled.

"Evidently, that ball print you made in the ceiling is still there."

Unnerved by the openness of his grin and the absence of their son, Jill reverted to safe territory. "You should have heard Turk Hostler's dad in the stands tonight, going on like his son's the second coming or something. I mean, please, he's not that great."

"He's a good pitcher, Jilly. We're going to need him."

"I just wish he never showed up."

"There's always going to be someone better, older, stronger, tougher. It's just part of the game."

"Well it's a stupid game," Jill said. She lowered her forearm till her fingers dangled at the corner where the arm of the sofa and the overstuffed chair kissed.

Clem brushed his fingers across hers. "Greatest game ever invented."

Jill stroked his softening calluses and protested with a sigh, "Everything happens too fast."

Stepping his fingers like a spider up her forearm, Clem teased, "Maybe golf would be more your pace."

There was no need to assess her readiness. She'd been grooming herself for this reunion since the day she and Gus had arrived. Pulling the throw pillow out from behind her head, she thwacked him on the shoulder and burst, "I'm not as bad as some people. Dennis's mom still doesn't get the thing where the batter can keep fouling the ball off on the third strike. I got that back in your day."

"Oh, that far, huh?"

Gripping the tassel like a ball seam, he let it fly. Jill countered. Clem snatched the pillow from her hand and pulled her on top of him, laughter rising up as if from some deep freeze—some lover's amber—the essence of the thing they once were released in its original form, gurgling playfully. He touched her cheek, her neck, her breast. She said breathlessly *not here*.

Taking Jill's hand, Clem led her upstairs, past the room where their son slept soundly, and into his own. The walls were painted a beigy rose. There was a giant cactus in a pot in the corner, and over the bed a watercolor painting of the arroyo near their home. There were no piles of clothes on the floor, no barbells, no scattered shoes. "Maybe there's hope for Gus after all," she smiled.

Clem led her to the bed, kissed the crown of her head, unbuttoned his shirt. "No more Gus talk."

The sigh was so heavy it rolled her neck clear around to one side, where, on the night stand, she saw beneath the yellow glow of a Mayan lamp, a framed picture of the three of them: father and son and Jill in the middle posed arm-in-arm in front of the Christmas tree. Gabby must have taken it the year before. Clem must have gone to bed every night looking at it. Gratefully, desperately, as if some apology were necessary, Jill burrowed her face in the cleft of Clem's chest. His skin smelled like grilled hot dogs; familiar, right. She laughed, warm air against flesh.

"What?" Clem smiled.

The laughter was suspended, the roadblock removed. "I thought you'd never forgive me."

Clem gripped Jill's arms till she looked straight up and into his baffled eyes. "Me?"

Closure came with a kiss, his lips, her cheeks, his sunburnt ears, until together they fell back, continued to fall, through the mattress, through time, he on her, in her, arms clambering at the night air as together they freed at last the long imprisoned words.

Lullaby.

Through the oak blinds in the room in which they'd made love, she could see the sun beginning to rise up over the hills. Clem was asleep on his back, lips parted slightly, one arm across his eyes as if dying content. Jill kissed his elbow and, wrapping herself in his blue terrycloth robe, tiptoed down the hall. Gus slept like his father, on his back, one arm across his forehead, the other dangling free off the edge of the bed. How often she had stood by his crib, studied his chest for the telltale sign of breath. No hint remained of that baby, that boy. His tanned face was now a study in angles and slopes; there was no more roundness, not even in his lips, which had spread out beneath a new line of darkening hairs. His brows, once as slim and narrow as Jill's own, were now thick as pelts. His nose had widened at the nostrils, his tiny perfect pores now clogged with tiny sacs of oil. His lips were parted slightly, pink skin chapped like soap flakes, and through his mouth the air traveled in and out, sated. There was not a line on his skin, not a crease of worry. Effortlessly he slept the sleep of a body well worn, wholly used. Jill studied his hand, the tips of his fingers, the pads of his palm. There was a callous forming over the bone just below his second finger. Bending down, she kissed it gently. Gone was the infant's reflex to curl up, to protect, the whole of her son's body now open wide to the world.

Dusting.

In the months that followed the midsummer night when Jill and Clem at last came full circle, the B side of the duplex became something akin to a giant storage bin. Old clothes, crates of wrapping paper, outgrown baseball gear, boxed bills, two-decades worth of *Sports Illustrated*, a 3-D model of DNA strands that Gus could not bring himself to dismantle, all were stashed in the space that became, day by day, less a part of Jill or anyone else. The only living piece she'd left behind was her study—her chair, her books, her desk, her lamp—which sat intact; enshrined. When she went there now it was only to dust.

Jill ran the rag along the keyboard, dared to touch the letters with her hands. Wrists sighing, she listened for the place where the words had stopped, for the memory of the lost tune. Hearing nothing, she began to hum. She'd known the song all her life. From the top of her childhood stairs, Jill had listened to it ascend like an organ chord from her mother's oven-warmed kitchen. In the absence of any greater certainty, she trusted that the notes would lead her home. Now, carrying the old tune like a baby in her arms, Jill rose to wipe the heirloom chair. With a blush, she noted that there was scarcely anything to dust.

Going, going.

Jill and Clem were married in February in the roughhewn chapel set back in the rocks of the monastery behind Gabby's house. The monk Gabby thought of as hers officiated. Gus, now a sophomore, (a term he was amused to discover meant wise idiot), read from Yeats as if he almost knew what he was saying, and looked happier than Jill had ever seen him—and she had seen him looking happy a lot lately. Just the week before, he had actually jumped for joy on the mound after holding a team of suspiciously-thick seniors to two hits and one run for a win in the biggest preseason tournament in the state. Scouts were there. Turk Hostler was not. Three D's and an F kept him on the bench for the first half of the season; by the second half, he'd simply lost form. Gus and Dennis shared Wilson's biweekly pitching duties, closing out the year with a respectable second place showing in the district. In the final game, Gus hit a home run clear across the center field fence— 390 feet. Jill remembered in that instant feeling like it was Gus himself that was flying over the field and out of their lives—going, going. There would be no glove that would catapult itself atop the highest reaches of that fence and bring him back. For all the time they'd spent looking forward, Jill suddenly wanted to look no place but straight ahead. Just this day, this hour, this fleeting smile. It seemed a worthy thing to record these moments with her whole heart, in sentient fullness, but for all it was worth, time passed just the same.

Perspective.

To the casual observer—a passenger on a plane flying over the Wilson High baseball field, say—it no doubt looked like a game. But to the mother of a ball-playing junior aspiring to the next level, it was nothing but a giant entrance exam taken over the course of sixteen weeks on a grassy, life-size stat sheet. Forget potential and a time for every purpose. Forget next year. This was it. The blank page on which all future chapters hinged. One bad game could derail a pitcher's earned-run average. One brief slump and the difference between a great batter and an average one became, on paper, indistinguishable. Every game was a litmus test, the results of which accrued in a heartless account, until in the end, after a 28-game season that spanned the months from February to May, the inhumane blanks at the National Clearinghouse for Student-Athletes—height, weight, ERA, wins, walks, strikeouts, RBIs, batting average, foot speed, arm speed, SAT, GPA, ACT—were all filled in, and no amount of love or care, not scented stationary, not mocked-up trading cards, could prevent a boy, from that point on, from being compared in the calculating eyes of the nation's most esteemed college coaches to the blearying spreadsheet of 60,000-plus like-minded players. If there was an advantage to having this insider information, it was not in the area of peace of mind.

Jill thought it best to keep her own stats. She made tally marks for the pitch count, and Xs for pitched strikes, and, in the event of any gray area, she used her own good judgment. In the season opener, for example, she did not see eye to eye with the scorekeeper on the alleged hit off her son in the top of the fourth. Clearly the ball had gotten past the second baseman and, clearly, the runner for the opposing team had made it to first; these were the facts, and they were not in dispute. But if it was also true that any reasonable person (and Jill was nothing if not reasonable) should have expected the infielder to catch the ball, then the hit was not earned by the batter, but rather yielded by an error and, as such, should defile the stats of the Wilson second baseman and not, as the official scorekeeper was suggesting, her son's.

In the folio-sized, leather-bound sketchpad she'd chosen to commemorate the notations of the season, on the perfect, white page with a hand-written heading Hits given up, Jill wrote nothing. Gabby cocked her head to suggest revision.

"What? He should have had that," Jill said, her hands guarding the unmarred page like a flame in the wind.

"The scorekeeper called it a Hit."

"The scorekeeper is a math geek."

Gabby studied Jill's eyes, her jaw, the hunch of her shoulders, which had not risen and fallen with the rhythm of natural breath since the first inning. "People are going to hit off him, you know that, right? People are even going to score."

308

With her Wildcat green pen, Jill underlined the heading in question, enhancing the brightness of the pristine page. 'Well I'm sure you'll let me know when they do."

At game's end, with Gus recording his first official win of the season and the record reflecting an impressive outing—10 strikeouts, one walk, and, two (debatable) hits given up—Jill capped her pen and exhaled. "One down, twenty-seven to go."

"At this rate, one of us will dead," Gabby mumbled.

"What is that suppose to mean?"

"Jill, I know how important this is to you—"

"Not me," she said, recoiling, "Gus."

"Yes, but Gus seems to be just fine—"

"What do you mean, fine? I think ten strikeouts is better than fine."

"I didn't mean his playing."

"If we had a scorekeeper who knew the difference between a hit and an error, it would have been a one-hitter."

Gabby recalibrated her breath to the length of the season. "It's an imperfect game. At the end of the day, the numbers are going to be what they're going to be."

Jill looked at Gabby as if she believed she already knew the outcome of Gus's life, and was trying now to prepare her. "Who have you been talking to?"

Gabby could not help but laugh. "Oh, Jill, stop being ridiculous!" Throwing her arms around her daughter-in-law like a blanket over a body on fire, she tried to shake some sense in her. "I just hope as the season goes on you'll be able to relax and enjoy the games a little more, that's all."

Jill rested her head on Gabby's shoulder. "I know, you're right. I'll try. I will."

"Good."

The respite of sanity lasted several seconds before Jill's head popped back up mid-thought. "We just need to keep him focused, that's all. Keep his arm healthy—"

Jill turned abruptly toward the post-game huddle. As if spotting a toddler in oncoming traffic she bolted, lunging toward the dugout where a team assistant was gathering up water bottles. "Gus needs his jacket on asap."

"We're going to ice him as soon as they're finished," the girl said.

"Find his jacket and get it out there to him now, okay." Jill stopped to consider the scoop of the girl's top and the impact of her proximity to the players. "And it wouldn't be a bad idea for you to put something on either."

Jill did not stay to see the girl screw up her face behind her back, returning to Gabby, who was halfway to the parking lot.

"Give Gus a big hug for me," Gabby said. "Tell him I'll see him Thursday."

A paint roller run from brow to chin could not have left Jill's face flatter. Hadn't she printed up special schedules just for this reason? Hadn't she laminated three copies, one for Gabby's refrigerator, one for her bulletin board, and a pocket-sized one for her purse?

"Wednesday."

Gabby turned her feet in the direction of the parking lot. "I'll see you then." Although she'd canceled her afternoon classes at the studio for the duration of the season, she still had students in the morning and the evening and on weekends, during the day. So much aspiration, none of it hers. En route to the car, Gabby realized she had an escort.

"He'll be playing first base," Jill prattled. "He usually bats better when he's not pitching, so that should help his numbers a little." The tiny muscles over her eyelids toggled and flexed like a pattern of buttons on a calculator. "Clem's going to work with him in the cages tomorrow morning. Says his bat speed needs a little tweaking or something. Nothing a few hundred pitches won't cure, right?"

Gabby opened her door and sliding quickly inside said, "He'll be fine."

Jill rapped on the glass and waved nervously. "Wednesday. 3:00. I'll save you a seat."

After the games, there were two distinct groups of fans. They waited in clusters on the opposite sides of the same double gates that fed the athletes from the field to the locker rooms. Jill stood with the other moms who, in the madness of their own pre-menopausal brains, tried to reconcile expectations with results. That left, on the other side of the gates, the friends of the players, a group that was increasingly, unnervingly, female. Flipping their collective hair back and forth like threshed wheat, they applied and reapplied their sweet, sticky glosses, giggling, always giggling.

So dizzying was their fruity morass Jill almost failed to notice the new girl who stood off to one side, alone, reading Kafka. She had the sort of daring bangs that cut straight across the middle of her forehead, a gash against pale skin, not unlike her skirt—short, too short—with too much white skin exposed. She was nothing like the tanned and tank-topped pool girls, or the shy, diminutive Latinas. Gamine and assured, she looked more like a beat poet, or the one girl in the whole high school who was content to stay home on Saturday nights painting wall size canvases in the nude.

"Who's that?" one of the mothers asked.

Another mother shrugged and stated the obvious. "Must be one of the new girlfriends."

The boys lifted their fists in the center of the huddle and shouted in closing, "Wilson, One!"

Jill watched closely as the team disbanded, sauntering in clusters by grade, by stature, by rank, back through the gates where the girls licked their lips and the moms waited annexed with burger money. The centerfielder stopped in front of the girl in the tiny yellow shorts and the tiny yellow top and slid his hands in her back pockets with a grip that would have served him well on the diving catch that came loose in the fifth.

Then there were the three girls in athletic shorts, chesty and bullet-thighed. The one with the tongue-ring, stepped forward to greet Dennis. The other two closed in around Turk, who had his own car and big plans in June.

And then there was one.

Peering up over the top of her book, her eyes kohl and certain, she locked down on the last of the approaching players, on number 21 and number 8 and, in the center, lucky 17. Gus had not even made it out through the gate before she threw, not only her arms, but her thin and nervy legs around Jill's son's body. Imagining the weight of her in his precious hands, which, at this moment, were beneath the skirt that covered precisely nothing, all Jill could think of was the strain on his pitching arm. Ten years she'd mothered the tiny fibers and muscle bunches that led from his wrist to his scapula, only to have it undone by the thoughtless impulse of some oversexed bohemian!

The urge to rip her off of him was countered only by the immobilizing forces of shame. All this time Jill had thought they were close, more than close. That there were no secrets between them. But here Gus was, in front of God and everyone, rubbing up next to a girl whose name Jill couldn't even begin to guess.

She must have been staring. They must have felt it. Jill could see the shrugs and nods, the winking brows that led the two of them, Gus and the total stranger, whose hand he was still holding as they approached. Jill wished she'd worn something more trendy. In her gray sweatpants and her Wilson Baseball sweatshirt and the cap she'd worn since Gus's first Little League season, she could imagine it would be hard for the girl to recognize that Jill, too, was a girl who could spin a web from the silk of her own mind. "Great game, buddy."

"Thanks."

Jill stared at the girl who stared only at Gus and waited.

"Mom, this is Jane. She's a friend of mine. From school."

Jane did not look Jill in the eye, but merely gripped the book in her one free hand, as if to explain herself, and nodded. "Hey."

"We have Honors English together," Gus beamed. "You should hear the stuff Jane says in class. Just makes it seem like some old story's the most exciting thing in the world."

"Imagine that."

What little there was to say had been said. The only thing left was for Clem to approach from the field, step into the circle, put his arm on Jill's shoulder like it was just another day at the ballpark, and reaching his free hand straight into the center say, "Hey Jane, glad you could make it."

In the head whips of maternal history, Jill swung early.

Distractions.

Where once there was no one, now there was Jane. Jane on the couch. Jane on the phone. Can Jane stay for supper, mom? We're doing our homework together. She was a fixture at every game, sitting, not politely with Jill and Gabby, but all alone on the top row of the bleachers, doodling disinterestedly just above the dugout in her silky little hand-painted wraparound skirt. Jill didn't even know why she bothered to come.

Suddenly a pitch went wild, caroming madly off the backstop. "You see," Jill said, "This is what I'm talking about. How is he supposed to be able to concentrate with her standing there like that?"

Gabby stifled a grin. "It's one wild pitch. With no one on."

"Still."

The next three pitches were all strikes: one fouled off, one a miss, the last, the batter caught looking.

"See," Gabby said, "He's fine."

"It's just not the right time, that's all. This year is too important. He's got to keep up with his school work, and his baseball, and then we've got the SATs in May— how are we supposed to get ready for those when he spends every free hour on that damn computer with her? Last night he was up till

315

almost one in the morning. You think that's enough sleep? I don't think so."

Gabby leaned forward into tented hands and pretended to need a better view.

Annoyed by her poorly concealed smirk, Jill said, "Don't tell me I'm overreacting. You felt the same way and you know it."

"And how did that work out for everyone?"

"Still..."

"Still."

"I'm just saying...." Jill countered.

"<u>I'm</u> just saying."

Jill readjusted herself in her stadium seat and continued. "Besides, it's not the same thing. We were already in college. We were of age for God sakes." Eyeing the black straps of the bra that was on full display in the torn open neck of Jane's cropped t-shirt, Jill scowled. "I don't get it. She's not even his type."

The ump called strike three to end the inning. Amidst a cloud of cheers, Jane moved from her spot, taking two baby steps down and across, down and across, sashaying her silky little folds in descent, down and across, till she arrived in front of Gabby and Jill. Jane reached out her hand; it occurred to Jill it might be to slap her.

"I'm going to my locker to get a sweatshirt," Jane said. She handed Jill a small, worn notebook. "In case Gus gets up before I get back, will you write it all down? Just the kinds of pitches, and the sequence, and what he does with them. He's really working on going the other way on breaking balls, so if you can keep that in mind, that'd be great."

Jill glowered. "I'm sure between the two of us, we can figure it out."

"How sweet of you to do this for Gus," Gabby said.

"As long as I'm going to be here," Jane shrugged, "I might as well help."

Jill watched as she walked away, her little hips swaying like a bell over her bare legs. In her left hand, the one closest to Jill, she was gripping, face out, title cagily exposed through the gaps in her delicate fingers, a copy of *The Inferno*. "Brownnoser."

"You better get it together, young lady," Gabby said, "Or I'm going to start sitting with her."

"Fine," Jill said, as if they'd been sparring like this the whole of their familial lives.

"Fine," Gabby said, and once again, tented her face to conceal a grin.

Deja vu.

There were, Jill knew, two kinds of repetition in a story. First, the use of repetitive words or phrases to create a certain effect, as in: he threw the ball again and again, harder and faster, faster and harder, day in and day out, game after game, the fixed number of throws in his arm ticking away like eggs in a womb. This sort of repetition, as any good reader knows, helps to animate a sensation; in this case, the weary throb of a pitcher's shoulder, the demise of a crowd-pleasing elbow, the dire stakes that rest on these two Achilles heels.

The second sort of repetition involves the reuse of events in the plot. Often, this is a sign of lazy writing, but on certain occasions (and a savvy reader will know the difference) absolute integrity to the narrative will demand that events recur. Take, for example, the night after the 23rd game when Gus arrived home so quiet it bordered on speechlessness. Mutely he pushed his pasta around the plate, refused ice cream with a grunt. He waved off even a call from Jane, grew restless during Sports Center, retreated to his room prematurely.

In his turbid wake, the question resounded: Was this it? Or was it just another minor setback in a future still as full of promise as it was before the silence— the ghastly, glacial, uncertain silence? In the case of true, organic repetition, even the writer will not know for sure.

We'll see.

There were four games remaining in the regular season of Gus's critical junior year. He sat out the first one as Dennis pitched badly and the relievers worse. He sat out game two, a 12-0 blowout in which his teammates grew mutinous; everyone's arm hurts this late in the season, they muttered. Wilson only needed one more win to clinch a spot in the playoffs. At home over the weekend before the final two games, Gus threw 20 pitches to his father in the backyard. Few but Clem would have noticed the way Gus shifted the source of his power to his shoulder, which inched, almost imperceptibly closer to his ear with each pitch.

To Gus's "Well?" Clem said only, "We'll see."

After the game three loss, in which Gus played first base and Dennis labored, again, on the mound, Jill found herself surrounded by angry, demanding parents.

"If we can't win without one injured player," she explained calmly, rationally, aping the speech she had heard Clem give to Gus the night before, "We can't win."

Her detachment was due in no small part to the relief she felt that Gus's stellar year-end stats were secure. Whether or not the same thoughts played into Clem's decision to bench him again in game four, Jill could not say.

Letting off steam.

On the night after the loss that kept Wilson High from the play-offs for the first time in twenty years, Jill and Clem turned in early. They did not make love or rehash the events of the day, the season; Clem was snoring before Jill finished brushing her teeth. She envied him that. Pulling the covers up over his shoulders, which had slackened in counterpoint with their son's growing fortitude, she kissed his cheek and turned out the light.

"McGaffey Sucks!!"

It was a shout to raise the dead. Jill and Clem bolted upright, checked the clock: 1:00 am. The howling taunts were followed in rapid fire by a drum roll of dull thumps. Clem ran down the stairs and threw open the door as the taillights disappeared with a shriek into the dark night. Splattered yolk dripped from the wooden sign that read Welcome.

"You should have let me pitch," Gus said. Clem turned to find him sitting in the dark with a bag of frozen lima beans on his shoulder.

"You would have hurt the team worse if you did."

"Gee, thanks."

Clem lifted the icy bag and pressed his thumb in along the seam of Gus's rotator cuff.

"Still tender here?"

320

Clem raised his son's arm up three inches. "How bout now?" Gus shook his head. Clem raised it to ninety degrees. "Now?" Again, it seemed fine. Clem lifted it all the way past his ear. Gus winced, sliced air though clenched teeth. "We're getting there," Clem said, returning the frozen beans to his shoulder. "Ten days you should be good to go."

For Gus the off-season was a mirage. An invitation to a training camp for Team USA had already been accepted; he was due there the day after school let out. After that there was the All-State Tournament, and a showcase at USC, and the Babe Ruth World Series, and a workout week at Tulane, and the Area Code games in L.A. in August. Clem filled a bucket with warm, soapy water and reached for a sponge. It was Jill's intention to help him but, standing now at the top of the stairs, she froze.

"Everyone says you don't care about the team. You only care about me."

"Losing does funny things to people's memories," Clem said, wiping the yellow slime from the door that all year long ballplayers opened like their own— for pizza or movies or replays of games, for a word from a pitcher who'd played an inning in The Show.

"Jane thinks you did the right thing."

"Jane's a smart girl."

"So why does mom hate her?"

The word rose up through the stairwell and slapped Jill

smack on the cheek.

"She doesn't hate her," Clem said, wringing the sponge clean. "She just worries about you getting distracted."

"Maybe I need a little distraction," Gus said. "Keeps it all from mattering too much. Know what I mean?"

For seventeen years, Jill had danced around the outside corners of the great But How? How did her husband—her son—stand stock still in the center of the madness and dazzle? But now, as if the curtains of Oz had been torn back, she could see: somewhere deep inside them there was an unspeakably intricate regulator and a funny little man with his eye on the pressure gauge whose shouts they could hear even above the steam.

"Yeah," Clem said, "I know exactly what you mean."

There was no maternal comfort that could compare to that. With a sigh, Jill tightened the sash of her robe and returned to their room, falling, for the first time in months, into a dreamy and effortless sleep.

The Catcher in the Rye.

The back of the Expedition was piled high with suitcases and coolers and bat bags and camera gear, and on the top, pressed flat beneath three rubber straps, two large clamp-on umbrellas for the seven long days they hoped to spend on the bleachers in Houston, Texas. Team USA was seeded second, and the week promised, if nothing else, to be the highest level of competition Gus had ever seen.

"Mom," Clem said, "All set?" Gabby was busily punching the buttons on her new CD player. Clem lifted the nearest headphone, and repeated himself. "Ready?"

Gabby raised her water bottle in assent and went back to her Vivaldi.

"Sip that slowly, okay. I don't want to have to stop every half hour."

Jill emerged from side A. She shut the door and tugged at the handle and, heading to the car, said, "Alright, let's get this show on the road."

"What about Jane?" Clem said.

"Change of plans." Jill stepped around to the passenger side and hoisted herself up in the seat. "We're picking her up on the way."

As if to bless the journey, Clem patted the hood of the car two times. "Alright then. Let's roll." It wasn't until he checked the rearview mirror that he noticed that the third row was completely empty.

"Where's Gus?"

Jill shrugged, jumped out of the car. Halfway to the stoop she returned for the keys.

Clem smiled, bemused. "Auspicious start."

There was no movement in the house, no hint of a body, no waft of cool air, which had been turned off for the trip. "Gus?" Jill waited for an answer, one second, two. She pictured the little man asleep at the valves, the pressure building out of control. "Gussy!" She headed for the stairs, hurtling them now, in the wake of his non response, three at a time. On the landing just outside their bedrooms, she met with his closed door.

Jill knocked twice as she opened it to find him lying on the bed, his head on a pillow, his knees propped up to support a book. Even from the doorway she could recognize the cover.

"What are you doing?"

"I'm reading."

"Well, we're all waiting down in the car. C'mon..."

Unable to lift his eyes from the page, Gus said, "Few more minutes okay?"

Now? When his junior-year grades were final and his SAT scores were all recorded and the whole family was sitting in 110 degree heat in a black truck, now he wanted to read?

"Sure. We'll see you in the car." She pulled the door

shut, started to leave, reconsidered. Popping her head back in, Jill said, "You know there's not really a catcher in that, right?"

Only then did Gus look up, and with a look of such literary haughtiness that Jill could not help but feel vindicated, said, "Yeah, mom, I know."

They'd be halfway to the Rio Grande before it would dawn on her that Gus's newfound love of reading had little to do with her, and everything to do with loving a girl who loved books. Jill could see it in his eyes, in Jane's, as she studied them in the rearview mirror, entangled and sighing from Tucson to Texas. From time to time she would shout to the far back seat. "What do you say we break things up a little, maybe play some twenty questions?"

Unhinging her lips from Jill's son's, Jane was always quick to oblige.

To the future.

By summer's end, the letters arrived like overkill: Rice, Miami, UT, Wake Forest, envelopes from the coaches of nationally-ranked Division 1 teams piling up like re-fi offers in their entry hall. Clem returned from the mailbox each day like a sweepstakes winner. "Here we go. Stanford," he said, waving the cardinal-logoed letter in the air. Jill looked up from table where she sat grading papers and watched for Gus's response. There was none. He didn't move from the couch. He didn't turn his head. Blinking appeared to be too much effort. What had begun as a much-needed rest had turned into a marathon session of Backyard Baseball played out without any apparent pleasure every waking hour of the day and well into the night. On the screen, the pee-wee sized Major Leaguers awaited Gus's next move. Sluggishly he waggled the controls and said, "Put it over there with the others, wouldja."

Run it out.

Fall was no longer fall, somehow. The leaves began to shed and the light to fade but for the boys of summer, there was no rest. Suiting up his weary bones, Gus took to the field each Saturday, each Sunday, for the last preseason scouting opportunities of his pivotal senior year. A stack of interest was no guarantee of a spot. Even as the bulbs in the pots by Gabby's front door dug in for their long winter's naps, Gus was expected to step it up a notch. Someone was always watching.

Gabe Hutchins had been a major league scout for as long as Gabby could remember. Perennially sunburnt and with a golfer's gentle demeanor, he had been with the Diamondbacks during Clem's final years in AAA-ball. Gabby had always suspected he played some small role in Clem's being kept on for as long as he was. Arriving late, she saw him standing against a rusted fence in front of first base, stopwatch in hand.

"Gabe Hutchins, as I live and breathe."

Gabe stood several inches above her, his broad, lean shoulders erect from a life of sport. He smiled and kissed Gabby's cheek. Even as they spoke, his thumb never stopped clicking as he timed each batter down the first baseline: 4.3 seconds or less and he'd give a boy an asterisk. Throw a bat and he'd run a black pen straight through his name.

"How's our boy?" Gabe asked.

"Which one?" Gabby said as Gus stepped into the box.

"I know how this one's doing," Gabe said, watch at the ready. "Hear about him all over town."

Gabby had kept her emotions in check for hundreds of Gus's at-bats, but somehow Gabe's presence made her blood surge unexpectedly. She touched her fingers to her neck as she watched her grandson swing recklessly at the first pitch and pop up for an easy out in right field. A single pop-out was neither here nor there: it happened to the best of them, happened more often than not. It was the trotting halfheartedly down the first base line, and the pulling off of his helmet before he even reached the bag that gave them both pause.

Gabe shook his head, clicked off his watch. "He's gotta run those out, Gabby."

Looking out across the crowded field she said, "Please don't write it down."

Leaving his pad in his pocket he smiled. "Only if you let me take you to dinner."

Gabby blushed; back in Atlanta they would call it a swoon. "I'd let you take me anyway." The words it seemed had been there all along.

"How does tonight sound?"

"Tonight sounds lovely."

A runner blazed past them, a banner of youth and speed. "How fast?" Gabby asked.

Gabe blushed and reset his watch. "I don't know. I missed him."

Resurrecting her best southern lilt, Gabby stepped away from the fence. "Why Mr. Hutchins, I do believe I'm distracting you."

The second time around.

In no time at all it was Christmas. After five years in the same small town, there were more holiday invitations than Jill had pants that fit to wear to them. "I can't believe it," she shouted, piling her old standbys one atop the other on the bed. "I didn't show with Gus till I was almost five months." Clem spread his hand across the soft, white flesh of her belly which peaked out like a triangle between two estranged halves of the same zipper.

"I like a girl with a little meat on her bones."

Sometimes new life can be detected in a single, innocuous thought. Slipping free of Clem's hand, Jill reached for the phone. "I think I'll call Jane. See if she'll go shopping with me. She has a good eye, don't you think?"

Jill was never one to shop in thrift stores, but Jane had convinced her it was folly (that was the word she used) to spend good money on party clothes she'd only wear for a few months. Like a schoolmate on holiday, Jane dragged her half kicking into the filmy, mysterious, space with rack upon rack of sleeves and skirts and bodices and pleats of fabric redolent of other people's lives. Jane worked the room like a party, touching each garment like the shoulder of an old friend. "How 'bout this one?" Jill shook her head, attempted to cast off those old, familiar batting-helmet qualms.

"What about this?"

Softening her grimace, Jill said, "I don't know if that's really me."

Afraid it was only a matter of time before she'd have to say yes to something, Jill placed her hand on the nearest hanger and began to search for herself through the musty racks. Arm after arm, silk upon silk, she touched the dusty, imperfect cloth, until, like incense, the wizened air began to seep into her skin, slowing her hands, softening her eye. She considered the merits of a rumpled empire blouse.

Jane smiled. "I like that song."

"What?"

"The song you're humming. I used to sing it in church when I was little."

Jill stared in disbelief. "I was humming?"

"You're always humming," Jane said.

This was not her life. Jill didn't hum, didn't shop in thrift stores, didn't even know what she was doing here with this girl she wished was not a part of Gus's life, not now, not yet. And still the tune played on.

"Now this is you."

Jane held up a dress that reminded Jill so much of something she'd worn the very last Christmas she'd spent with her family, she had to check the tag. Smoothing her hand across the blue crushed velvet, Jill smiled and did not say no.

Be thou my vision.

The jelly felt cool against her round, stretched skin. Jill reached for Clem's hand as the doctor pressed the ultrasound paddle against her belly. She could feel it on the inside, the gentle pressure radiating around her capacious womb to her spine, which quavered, as the room fell hush with the proof of life.

"Well, mom and dad," the doctor said, "Everything appears to be in order. The lungs look good, the brain development appears just right for 20 weeks. The heartbeat is strong and regular."

Jill turned to the screen where, in the gray fingers of ribs, she could see the throb of the tiny heart, beating, beating, as if endowed with its own big plans—as if the vision were already there, planted like a microchip in the nascent pulse.

"So," the doctor said, sliding the paddle around the left slope of Jill's stomach. "What did we decide? Do we want to know?"

"Looks like a ballplayer to me," Clem said.

"God help us," Jill replied, her head swiveling lazily on the pillow.

"Is that a yes?" the doctor asked.

Jill looked at Clem who could not take his eyes from the screen. "It's up to you."

332

"Whatever it is, it's perfect," Clem said. Only then did he turn, "But if you want to know..."

"I want to be surprised."

Entwining their fingers they shook one time firmly. "To surprises."

Just like that, the doctor flipped the switch and all evidence of the baby disappeared.

"Surprises are good," he said pushing back his rolling stool to rise. "I was sure I was going to be a firefighter when I grew up. Now look at me."

Tucking the knowledge of the sex of their child in his pocket with his stethoscope, he said from the door, "See you folks in four weeks."

Men!

Hard to conceive of just how much the world can change in four short weeks. As January turned a corner, Gus rededicated himself to his sport in a way that left no time or energy for anything else. Where once there was Jane, now there was no one. Not on the couch. Not on the phone. Jill couldn't say how long it'd been that way. She'd been so distracted, what with the pregnancy and her classes and the rush to finish the book before the baby arrived.

On opening day, Jill sat alone. Gabby, who'd closed down the studio without batting an eye and taken to accompanying Gabe on the road, would, she promised, be there with bells on whenever they were in town.

"Have you seen Jane?" Jill asked of no one in particular.

A klatch of girls tittered and shrugged. Their no's were thick with secret codes and the stuff of teen days that never made it home. Jill sat through seven innings, her eyes scanning the perimeter for late arrivals. If it weren't for the scoreboard, she couldn't have said who'd won.

"Gus pitched well," someone said.

Jill nodded. "You haven't seen Jane around have you?"

At the gates, Jill's stomach turned. There, where the girlfriends stood oozing entitlement was a busty, flat-eyed blonde as obvious as her undersized *Play With Me* t-shirt. Jill had seen her in the stands, cheering at all the wrong times. She knew the type. This was the girl who, in the fall, had bagged the quarterback, and in the winter, the captain of the basketball team, and now, as the school year was heading into spring, had her sights set on the star pitcher. Gus had no doubt caught a whiff of her in the hall, convinced himself in his testosterone haze that he was too young to be so serious about anyone.

At the mouth of the field gates, Jill watched Gus emerge and the blonde rub up against him in a way that could lead to nowhere but ruin. Gus spotted his mother out of the corner of his eye. Stripping the blonde's bangled wrists from his body, he left her in the dirt, crossing alone, approaching his mother with the guilty, charming smirk of the damned.

"Hey." He placed his man-sized hand on his mother's belly. "Did you see my hit in the sixth? Man, that ball was a wicked curve. Could you tell?"

Jill removed her son's hand. "I'm sure Jane would have really appreciated it. Where is she, by the way?"

Gus shrugged. "We're taking a little break."

"Oh. Whose idea was that?"

"What's the big deal? You never liked her anyway."

Every pore in Jill's bloated face stung. Tilting her chin toward the fence, where the men with the guns and the shades and the sweet tease of bright futures were gathered, she said, "Better not keep the scouts waiting," and, turning, waddled off.

I will speak.

Gabby rose early, as if the day required special attention. In the pale desert dawn, she laced up her hiking boots and stepped out into the morning air through which the June heat was already seeping. A lifetime spent on the sidelines of this game, she should have been able, on the day of the Major League draft, to look her grandson in the eye and say with certainty "You're it." But a lifetime in this game had taught her that projections were about as reliable as due dates: why an athlete achieved greatness, how a baby knew that it was time, these were mysteries that even pushing seventy Gabby could only pray to know the answers to.

She was winded by the time she reached the first hill where the chapel was set back in the brush. Across the lintel a verse was etched: "The desert will lead you to your heart where I will speak" Inside it was cool and nearly dark, and often her monk set a pitcher of water out for weary sojourners. Gabby took a seat in a pew halfway up. She made of her Wilson baseball cap a fan, and gazing through the flowing air, stared up at the cross upon which Jesus hung. It had always been hard for her to love this Christ. Only in Rome, where she and Gabe had traveled over New Year's, had she found her way. Standing spellbound before the *Pieta*, Mary holding the body of her broken son in her arms, the meaning of suffering at last took hold in a single, long-sought *yes*.

"I thought I might find you here." Her monk's voice resounded through the tiny space. It seemed strained somehow, as if he, too, were winded.

"I was just resting for a bit," Gabby said.

"Yes, yes, I know. You wouldn't want me to think you were praying." Lugging in his arms what appeared to be a dead monk, he dropped the bundled brown robe at her feet. "There."

"What on earth?" Gabby said.

"Did I ever tell you about the mysteries of 108?"

Gabby scooted over. She could feel the heat coming off his rotund belly, waited as he wiped his pink brow with a handkerchief.

"Well, as I'm sure you know, Gabriella, there are 108 beads in a rosary."

"Now, how would I know that?"

"There are also 108 beads in the Buddhist and the Muslim and the Hindu prayer beads."

"Really?"

"And do you know, my dear Gabriella, how many seams there are in a baseball?"

Gabby froze. "A hundred and eight?"

"Precisely."

All the cleverness was wiped clear out of her as she watched him rise again. "Here in this bag are all the baseballs you ever threw into that abyss."

"I haven't done that in years."

"Nope, but I've been saving them," he said. "My own little collection of sorts."

The bag was nothing more than a monk's robe tied up like a giant hobo's sack. Unknotting the corners, the balls spilled out across the flagstone floor, one after another, after another, each with the message scrawled in faded charcoal *Pray for Clem McGaffey*. Gabby jumped back as the dusty orbs rolled out across her ankles, down the aisles, under the kneeling rails. She gripped the back of the pew.

Rhetorically he asked, "What do you think? Shall we count them?"

Refusing, not the request, but the evidence, Gabby said, "No."

"Oh, yes."

Between the two of them it took three hours to gather up the 108 balls and move them to their final resting spot. Gabby's monk borrowed a wheelbarrow from the tool shed to aid them in the transfer. By noon, the fruit of their labor had taken form in a nearby clearing, the next generation of prayer spelled out in giant, round letters across the Sonoran hills:

GUS

First draft.

This was the last page. Whatever Jill had to say had been said. She lifted her puffy hands to the keys and, longing to tie things up in a red-seamed bow, went blank. In the living room, which was big enough now with the walls torn down, to house whole teams of gatherers, the guests had begun to arrive for the broadcast: Gabby and Coach Woo and Dennis and Ricky and some of the rest of the Wilson team, and two of Jill's colleagues, and the coach from U of A, and Mr. Urbino and Mario, who'd driven out from L.A. to share in the big day, and even, remarkably, Ned, Gus's first coach, who'd flown out alone: his son they were told in a letter at Christmas had died the year before of leukemia.

"Mo-om, hurry up."

It was all decided. If Gus were drafted in the first six rounds, he'd turn pro straight out of high school. If he went any lower, he'd play college ball first, preferably at U of A, where his father's number was waiting for him. Even in the best scenario—first round on his first pick team—it was still a long, hellacious road: rookie leagues, Single A, AA, all-night bus rides, all-day games, slavish pain with no end in sight, and bags of cold, cheap burgers shared with itinerant strangers piled four to a room as they elbowed their way to the top of the molting heap. What kind of mother would wish that on her son?

"Jilly, c'mon, everyone's here."

If only she'd started him sooner. If only he'd had more time with Clem. If only they'd had more time together. If only—

Like a slap on the cheek, the baby kicked. For the first time in the cramped final month, Jill felt its vehement presence. Thump! She placed her hands on her bursting belly. From Creator to created, the words flowed through her fingertips. *Be still.* As if, in that moment, a giant hand reached down over the crown of her head to play crack the egg, peace spread across her body. *Be still and know that I AM—*

"Mrs. M.?"

Jill's eyes rolled heavenward. Just to hear that voice again was enough to put her heart at ease. Torpid and content, she pushed back from the unfinished manuscript and surrendered the story. "You're here."

"I'm here," Jane said.

"Help me up, would you?"

With outstretched hands, Jane hoisted Jill to her swollen feet and, arm in arm, they walked into the crowded room to see what was meant to be.

About the author

Heather Choate Davis began her writing career as an advertising copywriter. Over the past 30 years, she's written screenplays, teleplays, one-acts, liturgies, and books—including her memoir, *Baptism by Fire* and the semi-sequel, *Elijah & the SAT: Reflections on a hairy, old, desert prophet and the benchmarking of our children's lives.* She's taught creative writing and created an original, arts-based vespers called The Renaissance Service™ She leads retreats at St. Andrew's Abbey, and speaks at book clubs and church events. Davis blogs at heatherchoatedavis.com and the Huffington Post about faith, family, culture, education, and theology. She has an MA in Theology from Concordia University, Irvine, and is the co-founder of icktank. You can follow her on Twitter @faithinwords. She lives in Mar Vista, CA.

33023086R00206

Made in the USA
Charleston, SC
02 September 2014